James
— the —
Lynchpin
of Our Faith

How the Brother of Jesus Jump-Started the Early Church

David Kitz

JAMES, THE LYNCHPIN OF OUR FAITH
Copyright © 2025 by David Kitz

Soft cover ISBN: 978-1-4866-2734-9
Hard cover ISBN: 978-1-4866-2736-3
eBook ISBN: 978-1-4866-2735-6

Word Alive Press
119 De Baets Street Winnipeg, MB R2J 3R9
www.wordalivepress.ca

WORD ALIVE
—P R E S S—

Cataloguing in Publication information can be obtained from Library and Archives Canada.

Thanks, David for taking the time to search out the pieces of the puzzle that form the life of James. Your book is a must read for anyone who wants to study the Epistle of James.

Carl Ruby, BTh/BA/MThS

I found this book fascinating. James, the brother of Jesus, appears in various places in the New Testament. David Kitz has joined the dots and offers a portrait of the man who led the church in its early years, and who shared not only Jesus' physical DNA but some of Jesus' other characteristics. The book is carefully researched and beautifully written. It is necessarily speculative in places, but convincing, and raises some serious implications for today's church.

Annabel Robinson, Professor Emerita in Classics, University of Regina

In this book, as in his dramatic presentations, David Kitz lives James. In *James, the Lynchpin of Our Faith,* David brings us along with him inside James' heritage, his thoughts and almost his very skin.

Don Hutchinson
Past Vice-President and Director of the Centre for Faith and Public Life
with The Evangelical Fellowship of Canada, and interim CEO for the
Canadian Bible Society.

During a period of bloody sectarian conflicts in many parts of the world, and racial tension at home, *James, the Lynchpin of Our Faith* is a major contribution. James, the subject of Kitz's carefully researched book, was a major leader and a cross-cultural bridge-builder for early Christianity to other communities.

Hon. David Kilgour
Human Rights Advocate & 2010 Nobel Peace Prize Nominee

History has often relegated James, the brother of Jesus, to obscurity, especially when compared to other early Church leaders such as Peter and Paul. Thankfully for the reader, David Kitz brings this central personality out of the shadows and into the light. Building on biblical texts, Kitz imaginatively reconstructs how James' jealous rejection of Jesus is transformed through an encounter with the risen Christ—an encounter that leads not only to James becoming the influential leader of the Jerusalem Church, but to his death for the sake of his brother and Lord. A thoughtful and engaging study of the life of James.

Derek M. Geerlof
Lecturer in Theology, Ambrose University, Calgary, Alberta, Canada

I love how David Kitz has let the Scriptures speak clearly from the beginning to the end of his book. Each chapter provides the opportunity to not only dig deep into the character of man that is James but also to go to Scripture for a fresh look at God's Word. I look forward to studying this book further with friends in and out of the church.

Andrew Nicholls
Men's Group and Bible Study Leader
Licensed Lay Worship Leader — United Church of Canada

James, the Lynchpin of Our Faith is a book written with deep insight into the biblical text. David Kitz sheds a great light not only on the life of James, but also on the life of Yeshua (Jesus), the light of the world. This book renewed my desire to read. Truly, I was drawn back to continue reading whenever I had to put it down. Thank you, David.

Noga-Aliza Abarbanel, Vice President and cofounder,
Ottawa Messianic Fellowship

David Kitz has done a masterful exploration of one of my favorite New Testament books, the Epistle of James. Having read many of David's previous books, I have become aware of his thoroughness and his comprehensive analysis of a biblical text. David makes you rethink how important James, and his epistle are to the very nature of our Christian faith. I recommend this book to those who are prepared to be challenged to look at James in a whole new way.

Rev. Dr. Ed Hird, co-author, The Elisha Code & the Coming Revival

Dedication

This book is about the relationship of two brothers,
so it is fitting to dedicate it to my own dear brother, Dale Kitz.

Contents

Acknowledgments

In the mid 1990s, I spent a pivotal evening in a darkened auditorium watching the Gospel of Luke come alive before my eyes. A one-man biblical drama had me totally absorbed. As the actor Bruce Kuhn held me in his magical spell, I sensed the Holy Spirit whisper, "This is what I want you to do with the psalms."

To my surprise that pivotal evening became the first of many steps that would ultimately lead to you holding this book in your hands. Of course, a great deal has happened in the interim, including the publication of a dozen book titles, four of them centered on the psalms. In addition to the spark that Bruce Kuhn ignited that evening, I have several people I should thank for their help along the way.

Chief among them is Wilf Wight. As I began my own one-man dramatizations of the psalms, Wilf Wight of the Canadian Bible Society played a significant role in arranging events and giving me much needed encouragement. He saw immeasurable worth in bringing God's word to life in this rather unconventional way. Without his help in those early stages, I am not sure if I would have persevered.

After a few years of memorizing and dramatizing the psalms, Wilf urged me to dramatize a New Testament book of my choosing using the Contemporary English Version (CEV). I resisted at first, but he persisted. One day while visiting the Bible Society store in downtown Ottawa, Wilf again urged me to dramatize a book from the CEV Bible.

I said, "I don't even have a CEV Bible."

"Oh, I can solve that problem," he quickly responded. And with that said, he grabbed a large-print CEV Bible from the shelf and hastily scribbled and signed his name to a note on the title page of that Bible.

The note said,

> To David Kitz:
>   I am expecting a dramatization of a book from this Bible soon.
>
>   Wilf Wight

He handed the Bible to me and asked, "Now brother, which book of the Bible are you going to do?"

I was stunned by his very direct approach, but without hesitation I answered, "I'll do James."

It took about eighteen months for me to get the epistle of James memorized and ready for presentation. Since that first dramatic presentation, I have "done" James perhaps as many as a hundred times in churches and community halls from coast to coast, as well as in the United States and Europe.

But I haven't just "done" James. James has done me. He and his words have gotten under my skin and into my mind and heart. After all, the letter of James is all about doing—not just believing something with your mind but truly living it out in your daily life. It's the living and doing epistle.

This book would also not have taken shape in the way it has without the influence of my brother, Dale Kitz. This book is chiefly about the dynamics of the relationship between two brothers—James and his half-brother Jesus. If I had no brother, it would be nigh-impossible to write about the differences, tensions, and joys such a brotherly relationship can bring. My brother has provided me with a rich background of personal experience. Thank you, Dale, for being my brother—a sounding board, encourager, and friend.

I appreciate the patience and dedication that Marina Reis and her team at Word Alive Press have shown throughout the publication process. I also need to thank my son, Timothy Kitz, for his services as the manuscript editor. Tim, you are a skilled professional and I am proud of your work.

Finally, I want to thank my grade one teacher, Vera Rathgaber. Yes, my grade one teacher taught me a valuable skill. Miss Rathgaber taught me how to connect the dots in the right order until a picture emerged. I got plenty of practice doing this because I repeated grade one. The good news is those connect-the-dots exercises bore some amazing fruit. I was only able to assemble a clear picture of James by connecting all the dots as his name appears in Scripture.

The book you are holding connects a lot of dots. In the end, I trust you will get not only a clear picture of James, but you will also get a much fuller picture of his divinely-conceived brother, Jesus.

Foreword

My acquaintance with David Kitz began back in the 1990s. During those years I was serving with the Canadian Bible Society. When arranging an evening program, it was one of my goals to demonstrate the relevance of the Bible to practical living. Is there any part of God's Word that better accomplishes this than the writings of James? David responded to my needs. He had memorized the entire Epistle of James and honed it into a powerful drama. The audience was always thrilled and challenged by his presentation. The book you hold is the result of years of study, memorization, and reflection by the author. You will learn and be challenged in your faith as you read.

If you were to ask your friends, I dare say most would admit a dislike for history. To extend that survey to a little-known historical character would have comparable results. And yet the book you are about to read will dispel that prejudicial attitude. The author has skillfully woven together relevant facts of history, archeology, and psychology into the context of biblical exposition. This breadth of thinking is typical of the author.

Though I am a lifelong Bible student, I confess to a meager knowledge of the character of James. His name appears frequently in the New Testament—but strangely, we rarely give him the significance he deserves. As the author develops the theme of James' character, we discover the reasons.

The reader will trace James' journey from unbeliever and critic to faithful follower of the Lord Jesus and finally preeminent leader in the early church. Beyond the Jewish population, he was instrumental in opening the door of the entire world to the message of the gospel. He left us a short but challenging epistle, reminding us that the gospel is not only to be believed but also to be lived.

This book will expose you to the seasoned reflections of a competent author and biblical scholar. You will be led along paths you had never considered. You will wonder why you had not previously considered James and his rightful prominence in the early Christian church. If you are a serious Bible reader, you will want to have your Bible handy–and a pencil—as you read and grow!

— *Wilf Wight, Pastor, Église de la Nouvelle Jérusalem, Vanier, ON*

The Closest Thing to Jesus

Dear friends,
> now we are children of God,
> and what we will be has not yet been made known.
> But we know that when Christ appears,
> we shall be like him,
> for we shall see him as he is.
> (1 John 3:2, NIV)

The Mystery in a Box

Who knew that a medium-size box could create such a stir? Archaeologists, academics, journalists, and theologians were intrigued. A debate raged for weeks about the authenticity of this ancient stone box. A sceptical public grew curious and hungered for more information. What did all this mean? What were the implications?

In the fall of 2002, the typical news cycle of war, politics, celebrity missteps, and market fluctuations was briefly interrupted by word that an ancient ossuary had been discovered. The inscription on this stone box read, "James, son of Joseph, brother of Jesus."

Did Jesus have a brother? Were his brother's bones once stored in this ancient ossuary? Who precisely was this James? Experts in ancient burial customs claimed that it was common practice to have the name of the father of the deceased inscribed on the burial box, but why include the brother's name? Jesus—Jesus? Was this the Jesus of the New Testament, the one revered by millions as the Son of God?

The list of questions grew. Scholars speculated, while public curiosity reached a peak. Israeli authorities questioned how this 25 × 50 × 30 cm stone box came into the hands of Oded Golan, a private collector of antiquities. Roman Catholic theologians chafed at the very notion that Jesus had a brother. Religious skeptics dredged up a variety of imaginative apocryphal scenarios.

Time magazine, in its November 4, 2002, edition reported that "Andre Lemaire, one of the world's foremost scholars of ancient scripts, announced that 'it seems very probable that this [box] is the ossuary of the James in the New Testament.'" Arrangements were made to have the James Ossuary examined by experts and placed on display at the Royal Ontario Museum (ROM) in Toronto. But alas, when the shipping container arrived by air from Jerusalem, it was discovered that the ancient stone box had fractured in transit. News outlets excitedly reported on this new ill-fated development.

Undeterred by these setbacks, repairs were hastily made to the ossuary, and the highly publicized exhibit went ahead as planned. Thousands flocked to the display at the ROM. In fact, the display curator at the time confessed to this author that no other ROM exhibit generated such a widespread frenzy of interest in all his years of service.

This stone box—this ancient artifact—may well be the closest physical contact we have to Jesus, the subject of the gospels. But storm clouds were brewing. Roman Catholic scholars dismissed the discovery on doctrinal grounds. According to long established Vatican teaching, Mary was a perpetual virgin. How could Jesus then have a brother? This teaching has persisted despite several passages in the New Testament which unequivocally refer to James as the brother of Jesus.

Some scholars questioned the authenticity of this discovery. Was the "brother of Jesus" portion of the inscription a forgery—a present day addition to boost the value of this artifact? Then there was the question of provenance. Where exactly was this ossuary discovered? Since the exact original location of this find was unknown, the context that archeologists rely on to ascertain authenticity was sadly missing. How did the ossuary come into the hands of Oded Golan? Was he simply an unscrupulous shyster out to make a fast buck by peddling fake or altered artifacts?

Golan's activities and his artifacts raised the suspicion of the Israeli Antiquities Authority. For years the Antiquities Authority had been attempting to put a halt to the illegal trade in artifacts discovered in the Holy Land. Here was a high-profile case that could send a clear message to all who sought to profit from this trade. On July 22, 2003, Oded

Golan was arrested in Jerusalem for allegedly forging and illegally trading in antiquities. But is the James ossuary a forgery? In a press release following Golan's arrest, the ROM stood by its initial assessment:

> Until the ROM receives convincing evidence to the contrary, we stand by our opinion that the James Ossuary is not a forgery. We had a limited amount of time to study it because of the amount of conservation work that was required after the Ossuary arrived at the Museum after being damaged in transit. The studies that were carried out on the inscription and broken fragments of the Ossuary, however, satisfied the ROM's investigative team that it was an authentic artifact with an authentic inscription that might make it the Ossuary of James, the brother of Jesus. There is always a question of authenticity when objects do not come from a controlled archaeological excavation, as is the case with the James Ossuary.

While the authenticity of the James Ossuary remains in question, it is the life of James, the brother of Jesus, which is truly intriguing.[1] The James of the Bible is far more than bones in a box. He was after all a living, breathing, flesh-and-blood man.

Present-day believers and church goers view James as an obscure figure, if they know anything about him at all. If Catholics are asked who the most important figure in the early church was, most would answer Peter. If Protestants are asked the same question, they would answer Paul. Yet if we could step in a time machine and ask Peter and Paul the same question, they would both answer James.

Over the centuries the historic importance of James has been overlooked. In the great gallery of early church fathers, typically Peter, Paul,

---

[1] For a thorough exploration of the James Ossuary and its implications for present-day Christianity, see Hershel Shanks and Ben Witherington III's book *The Brother of Jesus: The Dramatic Story & Meaning of the First Archaeological Link to Jesus & His Family* (Harper Collins, 2003).

and John draw the most attention. But James' contribution was truly foundational—even crucial.

Many may be surprised to know that the New Testament has a good deal to say about James, the man known to early Christians as the brother of the Lord. The time has come to put some flesh on those bones missing from the ossuary—to create a portrait of the biblical James—a man who had a monumental influence on the direction of the early church and by extension an impact that echoes down through world history to the present day.

It can be argued that James, known to some as James the Just, is in fact the lynchpin of the Christian faith. Without him the early church would have remained an obscure Jewish sect—an offbeat curiosity in the grand march of civilization. But due to James, the gospel message burst out of the narrow confines of the Jewish faith. It exploded across the Roman Empire and came to dominate the life and thought of the Western world for the next two millennia. Now with the rapid rise of Christianity in the nations of Africa, South America, and Asia, the time has come to take a closer look at the man who set this whole process— this train of events into motion: the man the Bible writers call James, the brother of our Lord.

— Part One —
James the Unbeliever
James through the Lens of the Gospels

---— 1 ——---

It's all about DNA

Have you ever wondered what your life would be like, if you grew up in a different family? I think we all have considered that thought. Maybe it occurred to you the first time you slept over at a friend's house. You thought, *what would it be like to grow up in this house, with this family?* Would you be where you are today? Now stretch that thought a bit. What if you were born into a different nation, culture or religious tradition? Would you still be the same person? What would you be like, if you were raised by a low-caste family in southern India, or by Masai warriors in Kenya? We all know that our home and upbringing influence our adult life in a thousand different ways.

Then there is the question of DNA. We also know that our genetic make-up impacts everything about us. Every cell and fiber in our body is programmed according to the genetic code inherited from our parents. That code determines more than just our eye colour and shoe size. It shapes facets of personality, disposition, and even subtleties such as our posture, the way we move, and the gestures we use. Of course the influences of nature and nurture, DNA, and upbringing were just as important in biblical times as they are today. We are who we are because of the complex interactions of heredity, family, and social influences. These same influences were at play in shaping the life of James.

It is only natural that, following in this vein, the New Testament begins by highlighting heredity. The Gospel of Matthew starts with a recitation of the lineage of Jesus. Incidentally, since they were half-brothers by blood, this also would be the lineage of James. And to truly understand James—to paint a portrait of him—we need to grasp the paramount role that his older brother played. With this purpose in mind, let's examine Matthew's account.

> This is the genealogy of Jesus the Messiah the son of
> David, the son of Abraham:
>> Abraham was the father of Isaac,
>> Isaac the father of Jacob,
>> Jacob the father of Judah and his brothers,
>> Judah the father of Perez and Zerah, whose mother
>> was Tamar,
>> Perez the father of Hezron,
>> Hezron the father of Ram,
>> Ram the father of Amminadab,
>> Amminadab the father of Nahshon,
>> Nahshon the father of Salmon,
>> Salmon the father of Boaz, whose mother was Rahab,
>> Boaz the father of Obed, whose mother was Ruth,
>> Obed the father of Jesse,
>> and Jesse the father of King David. (Matthew 1:1–5)

The gospel writer's purpose here is to establish the quintessential Jewishness of Jesus. He does this in the most organic way possible, by linking him back to the father of the Jewish nation, Abraham. Matthew's gospel is written to a Jewish audience and so by doing this, Matthew is saying to his fellow Jews, "Look folks, Jesus, the Messiah is one of us. Just like you, he can trace back his bloodline right to Abraham. We have a common heritage and here it is spelled out in black and white."

With the next portion of the genealogy Matthew takes this message a step further:

> David was the father of Solomon, whose mother had
> been Uriah's wife,
>> Solomon the father of Rehoboam,
>> Rehoboam the father of Abijah,
>> Abijah the father of Asa,
>> Asa the father of Jehoshaphat,
>> Jehoshaphat the father of Jehoram,
>> Jehoram the father of Uzziah,
>> Uzziah the father of Jotham,
>> Jotham the father of Ahaz,
>> Ahaz the father of Hezekiah,
>> Hezekiah the father of Manasseh,
>> Manasseh the father of Amon,
>> Amon the father of Josiah,
>> and Josiah the father of Jeconiah and his brothers
> at the time of the exile to Babylon. (Matthew 1:6b–11)

To the casual present-day reader, this list of names means next to nothing, but in Matthew's time every educated Jewish boy or girl would recognize that this is the full pantheon of Jewish kings. Here are the great and not so great leaders of the Jewish nation—royal heroes and scoundrels all. By providing this list Matthew has just upped the ante. He is telling his Jewish readers, "Have a look at this. Jesus is a royal descendant from the line of David. He is no ordinary Jew. Surely, he is marked for a higher calling."

Matthew continues:

> After the exile to Babylon:
>> Jeconiah was the father of Shealtiel,
>> Shealtiel the father of Zerubbabel,
>> Zerubbabel the father of Abihud,
>> Abihud the father of Eliakim,
>> Eliakim the father of Azor,
>> Azor the father of Zadok,
>> Zadok the father of Akim,

Akim the father of Elihud,
Elihud the father of Eleazar,
Eleazar the father of Matthan,
Matthan the father of Jacob,
and Jacob the father of Joseph, the husband of
Mary, and Mary was the mother of Jesus who is called
the Messiah. (Matthew 1:12–16)

Matthew has laid out this catalog of patriarchs to establish Jesus'
provenance. This is his royal heritage. To his Jewish audience he is saying, "We all know that the coming Messiah—the promised one—is a
descendant of David. Well, here is Jesus' family tree. He springs from the
right stock. He's got the *bona fides.*"

But did you notice that surprising little twist at the end? We are
introduced to *"Joseph, the husband of Mary, and Mary was the mother
of Jesus who is called the Messiah"* (Matthew 1:16). That's right! After
that great, long, monotonous list of *was the-father-of's*, there's an abrupt
change. Joseph was *not* the father of Jesus. The genetic link breaks down.
"Mary was the mother of Jesus who is called the Messiah" (Matthew 1:16).
Matthew goes on to explain:

This is how the birth of Jesus the Messiah came about:
His mother Mary was pledged to be married to Joseph,
but before they came together, she was found to be
pregnant through the Holy Spirit. (Matthew 1:18)

It's as though God is saying through Matthew that royal heritage
is significant, but it isn't good enough; the best human DNA isn't good
enough. It's only human after all. For the Messiah we must look to a
higher source—a divine source. *"But before they came together, she was
found to be pregnant through the Holy Spirit"* (Matthew 1:18).

God intervened. God put some skin in the game. If the redemption
of mankind was a rescue mission, then the Maker of the universe just
got seriously committed. He inserted Himself into the human genome.

Divine DNA—Holy Spirit DNA. Think of that for a minute. Divine DNA, the very nature of God, is linked with human DNA in the person of Jesus. *"She [Mary] was found to be pregnant through the Holy Spirit"* (Matthew 1:18). If you find it difficult to wrap your mind around that statement, you are not alone. Joseph had some difficulty with it too. In fact, he needed a bit of angelic dream therapy to convince him of the heavenly origin this pregnancy. Let's return to Matthew's account:

> This is how the birth of Jesus the Messiah came about: His mother Mary was pledged to be married to Joseph, but before they came together, she was found to be pregnant through the Holy Spirit. Because Joseph her husband was faithful to the law, and yet did not want to expose her to public disgrace, he had in mind to divorce her quietly.
>
> But after he had considered this, an angel of the Lord appeared to him in a dream and said, "Joseph son of David, do not be afraid to take Mary home as your wife, because what is conceived in her is from the Holy Spirit. She will give birth to a son, and you are to give him the name Jesus, because he will save his people from their sins."
>
> All this took place to fulfill what the Lord had said through the prophet: "The virgin will conceive and give birth to a son, and they will call him Immanuel" (which means "God with us").
>
> When Joseph woke up, he did what the angel of the Lord had commanded him and took Mary home as his wife. But he did not consummate their marriage until she gave birth to a son. And he gave him the name Jesus. (Matthew 1:18–24)

In a normal human pregnancy, the father's sperm, containing his DNA, unites with the mother's DNA in the egg to form a new child (zygote). In Mary's case, the Holy Spirit supplied the required male DNA, or its spiritual equivalent, to set the growth of the zygote (child) into motion.

Theologians have pondered and debated the topic of the virgin birth from the very foundation of the Christian faith. For unbelievers it is a huge stumbling block. How could this come about? It should not surprise us that those most intimately involved with this miracle—Mary and Joseph— would also have doubts and questions. They needed divine assurance and convincing proofs, even as many believers do today.

It's easy for us who live in a postmodern world to assume that the ancients of biblical times lived in an age of faith where everyone was quick to believe in miracles and the supernatural intervention of God. But a careful reading of the New Testament tells quite a different story. Many struggled with their faith. There are skeptics who demand proof in every age. But how glorious it is when the skeptic has his questions answered, his doubts stripped away, and he finds himself confronted by the living God. This was the case with both Mary and Joseph.

In Luke's gospel account, Mary's encounter with the angel Gabriel quite logically sets off some serious questions and doubts. We are told that "*Mary was greatly troubled at his [Gabriel's] words and wondered what kind of greeting this might be*" (Luke 1:29).

Mary had just heard that she "*is highly favoured,*" and "*the Lord is with her.*" If she found that angelic greeting disturbing, or as some translations say "*confusing,*" I am sure she found Gabriel's announcement which followed even more troubling.

> "Do not be afraid, Mary; you have found favor with God. You will conceive and give birth to a son, and you are to call him Jesus. He will be great and will be called the Son of the Most High. The Lord God will give him the throne of his father David, and he will reign over Jacob's descendants forever; his kingdom will never end." "How will this be," Mary asked the angel, "since I am a virgin?" (Luke 1:30b–34)

Mary's uncertainty is evident through her question. This girl without doubt knew about the birds and the bees and the normal ways and means that produce a pregnancy. Her question flowed logically from everything she knew about human reproduction. Would this promised-child come from her union with Joseph? That would certainly be the natural, predictable course of events, since she was already pledged in marriage to him. Can you imagine her surprise when she heard the angel's response to her question?

> The angel answered, "The Holy Spirit will come on you, and the power of the Most High will overshadow you. So the holy one to be born will be called the Son of God. Even Elizabeth your relative is going to have a child in her old age, and she who was said to be unable to conceive is in her sixth month. For no word from God will ever fail." (Luke 1:35-37)

Mary is unequivocally told that God would be the father of this child, *"so the holy one to be born will be called the Son of God."* This echoes what she had been told before she questioned Gabriel. Mary was told, *"He will be great and will be called the Son of the Most High."* Undoubtedly, it takes time and repetition to fully grasp the implications of such statements. In Mary's case it would take a lifetime. After all, this angelic announcement confounded her Jewish theology. How could God take on human flesh? It defied logic and the norms of human experience. While a Jewish Messiah was hoped for, even expected, who knew that it would come this way? From her own body no less?

To reassure Mary, Gabriel adds the news about Elizabeth's pregnancy. This aged, barren woman was the last woman among her relatives that Mary would expect to be pregnant. If the miraculous pregnancy of Elizabeth was possible, then perhaps this divine conception via a virgin was possible too.

Mary's response indicates the spark of faith was alive within her.

> "I am the Lord's servant," Mary answered. "May your word to me be fulfilled." Then the angel left her. (Luke 1:38)

Following this angelic visitation, Mary did not remain in her hometown, Nazareth, for long. Luke goes on to tell us that she went down to Zachariah and Elizabeth's house in Judea. We are not told why she made this journey, but Mary probably hoped for confirmation that Gabriel's words were true—that Elizabeth was indeed pregnant. If it was confirmation that she sought, it came upon her arrival.

> When Elizabeth heard Mary's greeting, the baby leaped in her womb, and Elizabeth was filled with the Holy Spirit. In a loud voice she exclaimed: "Blessed are you among women, and blessed is the child you will bear! But why am I so favored, that the mother of my Lord should come to me? As soon as the sound of your greeting reached my ears, the baby in my womb leaped for joy. Blessed is she who has believed that the Lord would fulfill his promises to her!" (Luke 1:41–45)

Elizabeth's words confirm that the spark of faith in Mary was sufficient. She had believed the angel's words—the Lord's promise to her via Gabriel—and as a result conception had become reality. As the gospel writer John puts it, "*The Word [Jesus] became flesh and made his dwelling among us*" (John 1:14). In the coming days, God would become flesh within the womb of Mary.

Later, we see that this concept of power residing in spoken words becomes a prominent theme in Jesus' ministry. When mixed with faith, the spoken word releases transformation, healing and the miraculous. Jesus speaks to the wind and the waves, and they obeyed him. With a simple spoken word, he heals the sick, restores sight to the blind and casts out demons. Time and again we hear him say, "*Your faith has healed you*," as the afflicted walk away in perfect health (Matthew 9:22, Mark 5:34, Mark 10:52, Luke 8:48, Luke18:42).

It is this potent mix of the spoken word and faith in the heart of the listener that brings forth amazing transformation. As it was at conception, so it continued through Jesus' life—words and faith formed an astonishing blend. His words brought life; God's word brings life.

Later we will see that James, the brother of Jesus, fully grasps this concept of power residing in the spoken word. It is a major theme in his writing, and he hammers it home like no other New Testament writer.

Is it legitimate to speak of divine DNA linking with human DNA to produce the God/man Jesus Christ? Deoxyribonucleic acid or DNA is a physical molecular structure after all, but the Bible asserts that God is a spirit. How could God, who is a spirit, have a physical component or discernible material structure?

If this question seems baffling, then consider this. For the last 50 years nuclear physicists have been trying to find the Higgs boson or 'God particle'—that elusive element that gives everything in the universe its mass. After spending billions of dollars on the Large Hadron Collider near Geneva, Switzerland, and then creating millions of subatomic particle collisions, scientists have concluded that what we call nothing (totally empty space) is actually something. The God particle discovery announced on July 4th, 2012, is the theological equivalent of saying that God has substance.

For more than two thousand years, Christians have been arguing that God has substance. He took on substance at the conception of Christ in Mary's womb. In an instant God took on human form. Godly characteristics found their full expression in a human form—first as a zygote, then a fetus, an infant, a child, an adolescent, and a man named Jesus. At every stage of development, he was both God and man. The essence and nature of God took on substance—a material form—and became incarnate. God was no longer only a spirit. He had a physical structure—a human form through which the world could see the express nature and character of God. As a human father expresses his nature and characteristics genetically through his offspring, so too the heavenly Father's spiritual code was written into every molecule and fiber of Jesus' being.

Furthermore, it bears noting that this God/man, Jesus Christ, was not a demigod in the Greek and Roman religious tradition of that period. He was simultaneously fully God and fully man, according to sound biblical interpretation and the earliest Christian conventions.

From a biblical perspective the divine nature of the child Jesus is undeniable. Jesus' biological father was God, as clearly stated in Matthew and Luke's gospel accounts. But why does Matthew bother listing his earthly, adoptive father's genealogy if, as stated, Joseph had no DNA in the mix?

The answer appears to be threefold. First, nurture matters. An all-knowing God recognized that Joseph would act as an ideal father to the boy Jesus. Joseph would raise Jesus in the faith. He would love and discipline him in a godly way and educate him in what it means to be a man in Jewish society. Everything we know about child rearing points to the importance of the father figure in the home. This is especially true in the case of boys. Joseph played a very significant role in the life of Jesus.

But Joseph played a crucial role in the life of James—crucial because he was the biological father of James. As the lives of these two boys develop, we will see the pivotal role this difference in DNA played.

Secondly, family lineage matters. In Western society we downplay the importance of family heritage. Rugged individualism is highly valued. But even today in Middle Eastern culture, a person's family name and lineage are of great importance, even paramount. An individual's life is always viewed in the context of family and family heritage. This is why such a high premium is placed on family honor. It is also why blood feuds go on for multiple generations, as families are locked into past modes of behavior and interaction. To fully introduce a person within such a society, one needs to provide their lineage. Matthew does just that by delineating Jesus' heritage at the outset of his gospel account.

Finally, royalty matters. The long-awaited, promised Messiah was to come from the royal line of David. This was common knowledge to all Jews of this period. Hence, Matthew begins his gospel with these words: "*This is the genealogy of Jesus the Messiah, the son of David, the son of Abraham*" (Matthew 1:1). Similarly, in Joseph's dream, recorded in the first chapter, the angel does not address Joseph as the son of Jacob, Jacob being his immediate father, but rather as, "*Joseph, son of David*" (Matthew 1:29). Why jump fourteen generations back? Simply put, it's because royalty matters.

Because royalty matters, it is the opening theme of Matthew's first gospel narrative:

> After Jesus was born in Bethlehem in Judea, during the time of King Herod, Magi from the east came to Jerusalem and asked, "Where is the one who has been born king of the Jews? We saw his star when it rose and have come to worship him."
>
> When King Herod heard this he was disturbed, and all Jerusalem with him. When he had called together all the people's chief priests and teachers of the law, he asked them where the Messiah was to be born. "In Bethlehem in Judea," they replied, "for this is what the prophet has written:
>
> "'But you, Bethlehem, in the land of Judah,
> are by no means least among the rulers of Judah;
> for out of you will come a ruler who will shepherd
> my people Israel.'" (Matthew 2:1–6)

Because royalty matters, jealous King Herod had all the male infants under the age of two put to death in Bethlehem and its environs. Clearly this newborn king had the endorsement of heaven, since the appearance of a star marked his birth. Furthermore, the scriptures predicted his birth. The crafty Herod immediately sensed the threat to his dynastic rule.

In Luke's gospel account we see that being a descendant of royalty mattered to Joseph. Why else would a resident of Nazareth make the long journey to Bethlehem for the sake of an imperial census, especially since his wife was in the final stages of pregnancy?

> So Joseph also went up from the town of Nazareth in Galilee to Judea, to Bethlehem the town of David, because he belonged to the house and line of David. He went there to register with Mary, who was pledged to be married to him and was expecting a child. (Luke 2:4–5)

As you can see, it's all about DNA—royal DNA—messianic DNA. It's all about being from the right family, the right clan, and being born in the right place at the right time as a fulfillment of ancient biblical prophecy. It's about divine DNA or its spiritual equivalent touching the right human DNA to trigger the birth of the Messiah—the God-man who came into the world.

But the DNA that the Holy Spirit touched to trigger conception was Mary's DNA. Luke provides us with a different genealogical list than Matthew as he traces back Jesus' ancestors all the way to Adam and finally to God. (See Luke 3:23–38.) He does this because unlike Matthew, who is writing to a Jewish audience, Luke is writing to a Gentile audience. Luke wants his readers to understand that this Jewish Messiah is not just the Savior for Jews, but for all humankind. Of course, Luke goes on to describe the stable birth, the shepherd's visit and the heavenly, angelic light and sound show that heralded the nativity of the Son of God.

Many Bible scholars believe that the differences between Matthew's genealogical list and Luke's list are due to Luke following Mary's line of descent, while Matthew follows Joseph's line. What is abundantly clear from both lists is that we are tracing the royal line of David, since at some point the lists merge and are identical.

Implicitly what both authors are saying by providing these lineages is that Jesus is the rightful heir of the Jewish throne. He is the long-awaited Messiah and the fulfillment of prophecy. His birth and arrival on the scene mark a turning point in world history. God has stepped into human flesh and has come to live among us.

The gospel writer John puts it this way:

> The Word became flesh and made his dwelling among us. We have seen his glory, the glory of the one and only Son, who came from the Father, full of grace and truth. (John 1:14)

James was born into this family, with this heritage, with this more-than-preeminent older brother. Talk about being overshadowed by an older brother! Like no one else on this planet James had the blessing, the challenge, and the curse of being overshadowed by the Almighty. And in human form, this Almighty was none other than his living, breathing, flesh, and blood older brother.

2

A Not So Immaculate Conception

James was conceived in the ordinary way—the way that is common to all humanity. There was no virgin birth for him, no choir of angels trumpeted his arrival, and no star appeared to signal his nativity. He was from what we can surmise, just an ordinary child, born into a very extraordinary family.

It should be noted that there are three men in the New Testament who bear the name James. Since they have the same name, the identity of these three men is often confused. The most prominent James during Jesus' earthly ministry was James, the son of Zebedee. He was numbered among the twelve apostles. He was the older brother of the apostle John—the John who penned the Gospel that bears his name. Peter and the two sons of Zebedee were part of Jesus' inner circle. During his ministry, Jesus often called Peter, James, and John apart from the other apostles to privately accompany him.[2] But there was a second James within the apostolic circle. This was James, son of Alphaeus. He is sometimes called James the Less. Though he is numbered among the twelve disciples, he did not play a significant role in the New Testament narrative.

In contrast to these two men, James, the brother of Jesus, was never part of the apostolic team. The apostle James, the son of Zebedee

---

[2] Matthew 17:1, Mark 5:37, Mark 9:2, Mark 14:33, Luke 8:51, Luke 9:28.

was martyred early in the development of the church in Jerusalem (Acts 12:1–2), and we hear nothing further of James, son of Alphaeus, beyond a mention in the gospel accounts. Our purpose here is solely to focus on James, the brother of Jesus.

But was this James really born into this holy family? Roman Catholics revere Mary as a perpetual virgin; hence, they view any teaching that Mary had other children by Joseph as utter heresy. However, other children is precisely what we find when we examine the New Testament scriptures. In fact, we have already touched on a Bible verse that disproves the premise upon which this Catholic doctrine is based. Mary was not a perpetual virgin, not according to the Gospel of Matthew.

> When Joseph woke up, he did what the angel of the Lord had commanded him and took Mary home as his wife. But he did not consummate their marriage until she gave birth to a son. And he gave him the name Jesus. (Matthew 1:24–25)

For our purpose, the key words in this passage are *did not consummate*. In other words, Joseph had no sexual union with Mary until after Jesus was born. It is interesting to look at how other Bible scholars have translated the original Greek of this passage. Here are some examples:

> Then Joseph being raised from sleep did as the angel of the Lord had bidden him, and took unto him his wife: And knew her not till she had brought forth her firstborn son: and he called his name Jesus. (King James Version)

> So when Joseph woke up, he married Mary, as the angel of the Lord had told him to. But he had no sexual relations with her before she gave birth to her son. And Joseph named him Jesus. (GNT)

And Joseph awoke from his sleep and did as the angel of the Lord commanded him, and took Mary as his wife, but kept her a virgin until she gave birth to a Son; and he called His name Jesus. (NASB)

When Joseph woke up he did what the angel had told him. He married Mary, but had no intercourse with her until she had given birth to a son. Then he gave him the name Jesus. (PHILLIPS)

All five of the translations cited above, while using different words, convey the same meaning. Mary remained a virgin until after the birth of the Christ child. Then after giving birth in due course, Joseph and Mary began normal sexual relations. This is what would be expected of any young married couple.

The King James Version (KJV) gives us the most literal translation of this passage. Matthew uses the Greek verb *ginosko*, which is translated into English as *know, knew* or *to know*. In this case, the verb is a negated progressive past tense, so in the KJV it is translated as *knew her not*. In the footnote to this passage the New American Standard Version more accurately renders the Greek used here as *was not knowing her*.

Matthew is using the verb know to convey the idea of carnal knowledge or sexual experience. By using the Greek form of this verb, he is harkening back to the first recorded instance of sexual relations in the Bible. "*And* Adam knew Eve *his wife; and she conceived, and bare Cain, and said, "I have gotten a man from the LORD*" (Genesis 4:1, KJV, emphasis added). Matthew's Jewish readers would immediately understand the biblical reference to this form of knowledge.

The chief point we need to recognize here is that Joseph's state of not knowing her came to an end. Mary was a virgin until some point after Jesus was born. In Matthew 1:25, the preposition rendered *until* (NIV) or *till* (KJV) is of crucial importance. It signals an action or a state of being coming to an end at a fixed point in the future. The Greek word translated as until is *heos* and it is more literally translated as *up to* or *unto*. In other words, Joseph's state of not knowing his wife Mary lasted *up to* the birth of Jesus. Thereafter, the marriage was consummated, as the NIV translation states.

Luke gives us further evidence that this marriage was consummated; he even provides a strong clue to the timing. After referring to Jesus' circumcision on the eighth day following his birth (Luke 2:21), the gospel writer goes on to report on Mary's purification rites.

> When the time came for the purification rites required by the Law of Moses, Joseph and Mary took him [Jesus] to Jerusalem to present him to the Lord (as it is written in the Law of the Lord, "Every firstborn male is to be consecrated to the Lord"), and to offer a sacrifice in keeping with what is said in the Law of the Lord: "a pair of doves or two young pigeons." (Luke 2:22–24)

Leon Morris, in his commentary on the Gospel of Luke, rightly points out that there are two religious rites recorded in this passage.

> Two quite separate ceremonies are involved here, the presentation of the child and the purification of the mother. The Levitical law provided that after the birth of a son a woman would be unclean for seven days leading up to the circumcision and for a further thirty-three she should keep away from all holy things (for a daughter the time was doubled; Leviticus 12:1–5).[3]

After the completion of this purification rite, it was deemed fitting and proper for a Jewish married couple to resume their sexual relationship. Because prior to Jesus' birth there had been no sexual relations between Mary and Joseph, one can logically conclude that their marriage was consummated shortly after this temple ceremony, most likely on the same day.

While the doctrine of the virgin birth rests on a solid scriptural foundation, there are no scriptural grounds from which one can argue that

---

[3] Leon Morris, *Luke—Tyndale New Testament Commentaries* (Eerdmans, 1984), pp. 86–87.

Mary remained a perpetual virgin. Joseph was instructed by the angel to take Mary home as his wife (Matthew 1:20). No special instructions on abstinence were given. One can then logically assume that normal marital relations ensued. In fact, in Matthew 1:25 we are explicitly told that Joseph *knew* his wife (consummated the marriage) after the birth of Jesus. Furthermore, Luke provides us with a definitive time frame as to when sexual relations began. Being observant Jews in every way, the Holy Family followed the rites proscribed by the Law. This includes the full rites of marriage.

It should then come as no surprise when we read that other children were born to this family. All four gospels refer to Jesus' brothers; two of the gospels list them by name.

> Isn't this the carpenter's son? Isn't his mother's name Mary, and aren't his brothers James, Joseph, Simon and Judas? (Matthew 13:55)

> "Isn't this the carpenter? Isn't this Mary's son and the brother of James, Joseph, Judas and Simon? Aren't his sisters here with us?" And they took offense at him. (Mark 6:3)

In the context of the two passages above, Mary is clearly identified as the mother of Jesus and his brothers: James, Joseph, Simon, and Judas. The Judas recorded here should not be confused with Judas Iscariot, the disciple who betrayed Jesus. This Judas—the brother of James and half-brother of Jesus—is widely recognized as the New Testament author of the Book of Jude. Jude is a Greek language variant of Judas. In fact, this brother Judas identifies himself in the opening line of his New Testament epistle with these words: *"Jude, a servant of Jesus Christ and a brother of James…"* (Jude 1a).

The Mark 6:3 passage is significant because it establishes that there were also daughters born through the union of Mary and Joseph, as well as four sons. The fifth son is Jesus, the firstborn, who, according to scripture and long-established church doctrine, was conceived by the Holy Spirit.

Typically, children are listed according to their birth order. This appears to be precisely what is happening in the above passages. The sons are listed from oldest to youngest, though in Mark's account Simon and Judas are reversed.

Since this was a patriarchal society, it should come as no great surprise that the daughters' names are not mentioned. They may have been born after the boys listed here or perhaps interspersed among the boys in birth order. Matthew makes no reference to the sisters, while Mark mentions them but does not provide us with any names.

This passage from Mark is significant for another reason. The townspeople ask, "*Isn't this Mary's son and the brother of James…?*"

In a patriarchal society—one that does not bother to list sisters' names—why not frame the question this way: "*Isn't this Joseph's son?*"

By referring to Mary rather than Joseph, are the townspeople tacitly recognizing that Joseph was not the father of Jesus? This is a culturally unusual way of framing the question of lineage. It is presumed that Joseph died years earlier and that may explain why there is no reference made to him, but nonetheless it is peculiar that his name is not mentioned.

The list of brothers provides another clue about James. James is the anglicized version of the name Jacob, or in Hebrew *Ya'aqov*. Jacob, the Old Testament patriarch, was the second-born twin son of Isaac and Rebekah. Jacob's older brother Esau was born with Jacob grasping onto his heel (Genesis 25:21–26).

Ya'aqov or James was a particularly fitting name for a second son in a Jewish family. But the name also suggests a certain character. The original Jacob was continually grasping for more. He was not content with his second-place status in relation to his brother. He provoked Esau into selling his birthright (Genesis 25:27-34) and later he conspired with his mother to cheat Esau out of his father's blessing (Genesis 27).

If in character and conduct James/*Ya'aqov* resembled his Old Testament counterpart, then in his formative years Jesus would experience very difficult and challenging times with his brother. As we will see, during Jesus' ministry James played the role of Jacob, a supplanter or deceptive usurper to great effect.

The list of brothers from Matthew and Mark's Gospels form part of a description of the same incident—Jesus' return to his hometown of Nazareth at the height of his public ministry. A closer look at Mark's account provides us with a fascinating glimpse into this messianic family and the interplay of hometown perceptions and dynamics.

> Jesus left there and went to his hometown, accompanied by his disciples. When the Sabbath came, he began to teach in the synagogue, and many who heard him were amazed.
>
> "Where did this man get these things?" they asked. "What's this wisdom that has been given him? What are these remarkable miracles he is performing? Isn't this the carpenter? Isn't this Mary's son and the brother of James, Joseph, Judas and Simon? Aren't his sisters here with us?" And they took offense at him.
>
> Jesus said to them, "A prophet is not without honor except in his own town, among his relatives and in his own home." He could not do any miracles there, except lay his hands on a few sick people and heal them. He was amazed at their lack of faith. (Mark 6:1–6a)

There is a kind of small-town-plausibility to this story that is quite disarming. Local boy leaves home; makes the Big Time, surrounded by adoring crowds and an entourage of followers. Our heroic figure returns home, but rather than adulation, he is greeted by small-minded jealousy and skepticism. This is a situation that in various forms has played itself out a thousand times, in a thousand small towns throughout the ages and in every society. Reading between the lines you can perhaps hear the crowd's unspoken thoughts. "He's nothing special. I remember him as a runny-nosed little kid. We know his family. There's nothing wonderful about them. Who does he think he is?" This outcome was to be expected. They had no faith in him. He was too familiar, too ordinary in their eyes. They were amazed at his wisdom and the reports of miracles, but in their eyes he had committed the sin of overreaching. He had gone well beyond the expected small-town norms. Over achievers must be put in their place, so "*they took offence at him*" (Matthew 13:57a; Mark 6:3b).

There's a confounding mix of the ordinary meeting the highly extraordinary in this account—an encounter of the common man with the ultimate superhuman. And Jesus was both: common and supernatural. He was the carpenter turned Savior of the world. This hometown reaction is what you might expect when God takes on flesh and becomes one of us. No one knew quite how to handle Him. He does not fit the norm. He is incongruent in so many ways, far outside the norm of human experience. The easiest response is to reject Him.

What can we conclude about James, the subject of this book, from these observations? What we have portrayed here is a rather ordinary first-century Jewish family. James, the second son of Joseph the carpenter (Matthew 13:55), was conceived and came into the world through Mary in the same way as any other child on the planet. He had one older brother named Jesus and three younger brothers, in addition to at least two sisters. It seems clear that Joseph had passed away at some point before the hometown visit recorded in Mark 6:1–6 and Matthew 13: 53–58. Before taking up his public ministry, Jesus had worked in the family business as a carpenter. It seems highly likely that with Jesus' departure, James would have continued in the family trade. It is equally clear that the townspeople of Nazareth largely rejected Jesus' ministry. They had no faith in him and "*took offence at him*" (Matthew 13:57a; Mark 6:3b).

So how did James respond to his brother's rise to fame? As we will see, James, like those around him, showed himself to be a true hometown boy, a son of Nazareth. He too shared in their skepticism.

———— 3 ————

Who am I? The Defining Question

Iohn in the opening chapter to his gospel account makes this observation about Jesus: "*He was in the world, and though the world was made through him, the world did not recognize him. He came to that which was his own, but his own did not receive him*" (John 1:10–11).

Most commentators on this passage conclude that John, who wrote this gospel in the latter part of the first century, was referring to the rejection of Jesus by the majority of the Jewish nation. To paraphrase: Jesus came to his own people, but they did not recognize him as their Messiah or receive him as such.

Undoubtedly, this is a correct interpretation of this passage. However, I would argue that typically we view and interpret this passage much too broadly. On the macro level this standard view is correct; Jesus was rejected by the Jewish nation. But it is within the microcosm of the family that the truth of this passage truly hits home. Jesus was not only rejected by his nation; he was rejected by his own family. A careful reading of the gospels makes this painful point clear.

The hometown rejection, which we read of in the previous chapter, foreshadows a much more extensive rejection of Jesus that rippled through his family, through the religious establishment and the whole of Jewish society. It culminated in his condemnation by the Sanhedrin and crucifixion at the hands of the Romans. Despite his wise teachings, which were coupled with signs and wonders, most of his contemporaries did not recognize the divinity of Christ. In their eyes, he was just a man—a man dangerously masquerading as so much more. The Gospel accounts make it blatantly clear that this was also the view that James and his brothers held.

But before we delve deeper into Jesus' rejection by his family, we need to examine the topic of self-recognition. In the quote above, John stated, *"He [Jesus] was in the world, and though the world was made through him, the world did not recognize him"* (John 1:10).

John sees the problem of Jesus rejection as stemming from a failure of the people to recognize who he was. John clearly saw Jesus as the Creator of the universe; he recognized Jesus as Deity, but by and large Jewish society did not. He was Deity disguised in humanity and for many the disguise was too effective, too confounding. To this day it remains a stumbling block, particularly for those trained in the Jewish faith. God taking on human form is a foreign concept, and it is incomprehensible.

Now imagine for a moment how baffling—how incomprehensible—this concept would be for a twelve-year-old Jewish boy. But somehow at the age of twelve, Jesus grasped it. He recognized his own Deity. He saw himself as the Son of God. How exactly did this come about?

Childhood is all about self-discovery and learning our place in the world. Quite naturally self-discovery begins at home within the context of the family. We learn who we are from our parents and siblings. They define our genetic and cultural heredity. Genetically we are like them, and we become even more like them through our exposure to their loving nurture, interaction and instruction. Our family defines us, particularly at a young age. But for reasons we do not fully understand, Jesus saw himself as radically different. He saw that he did not fit or rightfully belong in his father's household—in Joseph's household. Already at age twelve, he recognized that he was not Joseph's son.

How did this come about? How did Jesus come to see himself as different? Furthermore, it is one thing to conclude that this man you have grown up with is not your true father, but it is a huge leap for a twelve-year-old to conclude that he is some kind of divinely conceived genetic mutant, an offspring of God—a God/Boy. Yet that is how Jesus came to see himself.

The only gospel account of Jesus' childhood presents a fascinating snapshot of Jesus' self-perception. In the following account, Jesus reveals how he sees himself; he grasps his true identity:

> Every year Jesus' parents went to Jerusalem for the Festival of the Passover. When he was twelve years old, they went up to the festival, according to the custom. After the festival was over, while his parents were returning home, the boy Jesus stayed behind in Jerusalem, but they were unaware of it. Thinking he was in their company, they traveled on for a day. Then they began looking for him among their relatives and friends. When they did not find him, they went back to Jerusalem to look for him. After three days they found him in the temple courts, sitting among the teachers, listening to them and asking them questions. Everyone who heard him was amazed at his understanding and his answers. When his parents saw him, they were astonished. His mother said to him, "Son, why have you treated us like this? Your father and I have been anxiously searching for you."
>
> "Why were you searching for me?" he asked. "Didn't you know I had to be in my Father's house?" But they did not understand what he was saying to them.
>
> Then he went down to Nazareth with them and was obedient to them. But his mother treasured all these things in her heart. And Jesus grew in wisdom and stature, and in favor with God and man. (Luke 2:41–52)

Jesus response to Mary's question speaks volumes about Jesus' self-perception. "*Why were you searching for me? Didn't you know I had to be in my Father's house?*"

It's almost as though he is saying to his mother, "I know who I am. I've figured it out. Did you forget whose son I really am? God is my Father. All I wanted to do is spend some time with Him."

"But they did not understand what he was saying to them" (Luke 2:50).

If Mary and Joseph did not understand what Jesus was saying to them, it would seem to indicate that they did not tell him of his divine origin. There was no private conversation where Joseph took Jesus aside and said, "Look son, you're really not my son. Oh, and by the way, this is how you came about..."

Apparently, Mary did not have this conversation with Jesus either. Think about it. It would be a very difficult conversation to initiate. Explaining the virgin birth would surely stretch the bounds of common logic and would profoundly conflict with the norms of the Jewish faith. Why would the one true God impregnate a Jewish girl by the Spirit? Consider it for a moment. It's preposterous and intrinsically it runs counter to all we know of Jewish religious dogma.

How do you tell your firstborn that he is the Son of God? Apparently, you don't. If he truly is the Son of God, you let him figure it out. From this account, it would seem this is the course of inaction that Mary and Joseph took. They let Jesus figure it out. And he did.

That's what's truly remarkable about this account. The twelve-year-old figured it out. He discovered his true identity.

The question remains: How did Jesus do it? How did he come to realize his divinity?

Typically, we read this account of the lost twelve-year-old Jesus from the viewpoint of a parent. We identify with the stress of losing a child in a big city. We would title this story, "Mary and Joseph find lost Jesus." But the story reads quite differently when we view it from the perspective of a child trying to discover who he really is. Viewed from Jesus' perspective the title of the story might well be, "Lost Boy finds Himself" or "Lost Boy Discovers His Divinity."

How did Jesus discover he was God's son? Some believers might well reason that the answer is obvious. Jesus is God; therefore, he is omniscient. The all-knowing Jesus would surely know that he was God's son. But many theologians would beg to differ. They view the humanity of

Christ as all-pervasive. Jesus was 100% human, and as such he needed to learn and discover his identity, even as any child does. The apostle Paul's writing lends credence to this perspective. Here is his advice to the believers at Philippi:

> In your relationships with one another, have the same mindset as Christ Jesus:
> Who, being in very nature God, did not consider equality with God something to be used to his own advantage;
> rather, he made himself nothing by taking the very nature of a servant, being made in human likeness.
> And being found in appearance as a man, he humbled himself by becoming obedient to death—even death on a cross!
> Therefore God exalted him to the highest place and gave him the name that is above every name,
> that at the name of Jesus every knee should bow, in heaven and on earth and under the earth,
> and every tongue acknowledge that Jesus Christ is Lord, to the glory of God the Father. (Philippians 2:5–11)

The passage above contrasts the humility and exaltation of Christ. In taking on humanity, Christ emptied himself of Deity. He fully became one of us. He was faced with the same frailties and limitations. In other words, in his humanity, he did not know everything. His feet got tired after a long day, and, yes, they probably stank too. He was fully human. He grew hungry and thirsty, and he was tempted in every way just as we are.

The writer of the Book of Hebrews, when speaking of Jesus tells us that he was

> fully human in every way, in order that he [Jesus] might become a merciful and faithful high priest in service to

God, and that he might make atonement for the sins of the people. Because he himself suffered when he was tempted, he is able to help those who are being tempted. (Hebrews 2:17–18)

If this is true, then the boy Jesus needed to discover his divine identity. It may have been written into every fibre of his being, but he still needed to discover it, just as any young musical prodigy needs to explore and discover his or her gift. All divine gifts must be discovered and developed to reach their maximum potential.

Luke concludes his boyhood account about Jesus with these words: *"Jesus grew in wisdom and stature, and in favor with God and man"* (Luke 2:41–52). Evidently, there was a process of learning and growth in Jesus' development, even as there is in any boy transitioning to manhood. But there was something different about this child. His interests were different from his peers. We are told that he was found in the temple courts, *"sitting among the teachers, listening to them and asking them questions. Everyone who heard him was amazed at his understanding and his answers"* (Luke 2:46b–47). Clearly, he possessed wisdom and insight beyond his years. His divine DNA was showing. It was written into the very character of his soul, and he was learning to read what was written there.

He was the Son of God.

That is what the boy Jesus saw writ large upon his life. That is what he heard his Father saying to him. If Joseph did not tell the boy Jesus about his divine origin, his heavenly Father certainly did. He was whispering in his ear, "You are my son!"

The teachers were amazed because they were catching glimpses of Deity.

Why did this realization of who he was occur to Jesus at this time?

Developmental psychologists tell us there is something quite significant about the mind of a twelve-year-old. For most children it's the year of the great leap forward. Mentally there is this massive shift that takes place in brain function. The brain moves from concrete to abstract thought. Ideas take on far greater significance. The mind is less dependent on physical objects as props to thought. Ideas and concepts can be grasped and manipulated in ways that were impossible a few months earlier. In this context, the concept and understanding of self takes on a new significance.

In his twelfth year, for the first time Jesus fully understood who he was.

Jesus was different from his brothers. That was probably the first clue in discovering his true identity. We don't know what Jesus looked like. First century people didn't have cameras, and Da Vinci and the European master artists did not have time machines, so we really have no clear idea about Jesus' appearance.

We do not know what divine DNA looks like when it takes on human form. Did Jesus simply look like a male version of Mary? Or were there other marked differences in appearance coming from the heavenly Father?

We can safely assume that Jesus didn't look like Joseph, and if he didn't resemble Joseph, he probably appeared to be different from his half-brothers, James, Joseph, Simon, and Jude. A father's facial and physical traits are usually very evident in his sons.

A perceptive child would notice the differences. And Jesus was a perceptive child. By age twelve he would recognize that he was the different one, the odd one in the family. Knowing whose child you are cuts to the very core of your identity. Discovering you are not who you think you are is jarring to say the least. Imagine waking up to this totally altered reality. You are not your father's son. You belong to someone else. You are someone else.

That is the reality that the twelve-year-old Jesus was coming to grips with. His decision to not return to Nazareth with his parents needs to be viewed in this context. Was this a deliberate decision? If Jesus knew he was not Joseph's son, why return with this man who was not his father? But if he wasn't Joseph's son, whose child was he? Did Jesus stay in Jerusalem in an attempt to discover the answer to that question? The twelve-year-old Jesus was coming face to face with an intense identity crisis.

There is a huge level of pathos and emotional freight in this story. Joseph and Mary are frantically worried and searching for their lost son. But on the other side of the equation, we see a lost son—with his whole sense of self in question. Was he searching for and discovering a new identity? But there is a huge leap from recognizing you are different—not fully one of the family—to identifying yourself as the Son of God.

But Jesus made that leap. The New King James Version translates Jesus' response to Mary's question in the temple this way. *"Why did you seek Me? Did you not know that I must be about My Father's business?"* (Luke 2:49).

Implicit in that response is Jesus' recognition that he was not the carpenter's son, but instead God's son—God's son ready and willing to take on God's work.

The easier conclusion a perceptive twelve-year-old might reach is that he was the product of Mary's union with another man—maybe the result of a teenage fling or indiscretion, or perhaps Mary was raped by a Roman soldier. That would account for Jesus' apparent differences from the other members in the family. It might also be the reason why these differences were not discussed. His conception was an embarrassing episode prior to marriage. For reasons of family pride, some things were better left unsaid.

But Jesus did not reach this more mundane conclusion. According to the scenario presented here, everything within him told him he was the Son of God. His internal script contained a different code, and there in the temple he had deciphered it. He was God's son come in the flesh. The lost boy had found Himself. He had found His true identity, not as Joseph's son, but as God's Son.[4]

Time would tell if this was just the deluded thoughts of a preteen dreamer, or if there was the ring of truth to his self-identification with Deity.

J. W. Shepard in his classic *The Christ of the Gospels* gives us his take on this account from Luke:

> Theologians have speculated as to when Jesus first became conscious of the fact that He was God's son in a peculiar sense and of his Messianic mission. We turn to

---

[4] A more commonly accepted scenario for Jesus' self-identification is presented in the next chapter.

these words as the sole clear self-revelation of Jesus in his boyhood years. In them we find his feeling of a distinct disappointment, that his parents did not understand Him better. He reveals in them the consciousness of a unique relationship to His Father. He expressed in them a clear sense of His primary obligations to God, which for the time had so engrossed His attention, that He almost lost sight of time and his human filial relationships.[5]

At this point readers may well be questioning how this connects with James. This is supposed to be a book about James after all. But James may well have been present—standing next to Mary and Joseph when Jesus said *"Why did you seek Me? Did you not know that I must be about My Father's business?"* (Luke 2:49 NKJV)

There are some sound reasons for believing that this was the case—that young James was present when Jesus identified himself as God's son. In the previous chapter we clearly established that there were other children born to Mary and Joseph. Luke tells us that… "Every year Jesus' parents went to Jerusalem for the Festival of the Passover. When he was twelve years old, they went up to the festival, according to the custom" (Luke 2:41–42).

It is logical to assume that this was a pilgrimage that the whole family undertook. Being observant Jews, there are no obvious grounds to assume otherwise. If this is the case, there may well have been as many as five or six children in this family entourage. In this context losing track of one child makes far more sense, given the large size of this family. The oldest boy, Jesus, was more independent, so *"Thinking he was in their company, they traveled on for a day. Then they began looking for him among their relatives and friends"* (Luke 2:44).

When Joseph and Mary returned to Jerusalem to search for Jesus, James and his brothers and sisters may have come with them. Having just lost one child, Mary and Joseph would want their remaining children close beside them, or safe in the care of the extended family. Hence,

---

[5] J. W. Shepard, *The Christ of the Gospels* (Eerdmans, 1938), p. 54.

it is possible that James was present with his parents when they came upon Jesus in the temple courts.

Finally, we need to consider how this story came to be in Luke's Gospel. In the introduction to his gospel, the good doctor Luke gives us some insight into the sources he drew upon when he wrote his account of Jesus life.

> Many have undertaken to draw up an account of the things that have been fulfilled among us, just as they were handed down to us by those who from the first were eyewitnesses and servants of the word. With this in mind, since I myself have carefully investigated everything from the beginning, I too decided to write an orderly account for you, most excellent Theophilus, so that you may know the certainty of the things you have been taught. (Luke 1:1–4)

Luke asserts that he did some careful investigation, and from the above statement it is reasonable to assume that he interviewed eyewitnesses before he sat down to write this portion of his Gospel account. Who were these eyewitnesses?

Luke tells us more about the birth of Jesus and John the Baptist than any other Gospel writer. He alone describes the stable birth in Bethlehem, the angelic visitation and the adoration of the shepherds. He alone speaks of the encounter with Simeon and the prophetess Anna in the temple courts, where Mary and Joseph hear prophetic words spoken over the baby Jesus. None of the other three Gospel writers make mention of the boyhood of Jesus. Only Luke recounts the twelve-year-old Jesus' instructional escapade with the teachers of the law in the temple courts.

There is a richness of detail in these stories which strongly suggests that Luke got these accounts from someone who was present when they happened, someone who had an intimate knowledge of the holy family and their history. Two possible sources spring immediately to mind: Mary and James.

Since Joseph died at a relatively young age, Mary would appear to be the obvious choice. But if Luke had an opportunity to speak with her, she would be well-advanced in years. When was Luke's Gospel written? Could Luke have interviewed Mary or James—or perhaps both—before he penned his Gospel?

Biblical scholars vary widely in their dating of Luke's Gospel. In his introduction to the Book of Luke, Dr. J. Lyle Story, Associate Professor of Biblical Studies at Regent University, makes the following statement:

> Since Luke was in Caesarea during Paul's two-year incarceration there (Acts 27:1), he would have had ample opportunity during that time to conduct the investigation he mentions in Luke 1:1–4. If this is the case, then Luke's Gospel may be dated around A.D. 59–60, but as late as A.D. 75.[6]

It is by no means unreasonable to picture a seventy-five-year-old Mary in the company of her greying son, James, sitting down over a meal with the good doctor Luke to discuss the events of Jesus' birth and childhood. It is in fact a thoroughly plausible explanation as to how Luke was able to provide us with such a vivid account of these gospel events. Luke interviewed, probed and questioned the eyewitnesses that were available to him. And who would be better to question about Christ's birth than Mary, the mother of Jesus?

In summing up Jesus' birth and the visitation of the shepherds, Luke wrote, "*But Mary treasured up all these things and pondered them in her heart*" (Luke 2:19). Since these are inner thoughts, how would Luke know that this was so, unless Mary told him?

Some would argue these passages simply came through the divine inspiration that was at work when Luke penned these words—an inspiration that infuses all the holy scriptures. But Luke clearly states that his sources were eyewitnesses. The use of eyewitness accounts does not

---

[6] J. Lyle Story, "Introduction: The Gospel of Luke," *Spirit Filled Life Bible, New King James Version,* General Editor Jack W. Hayford (Thomas Nelson, 1991), p. 1503.

nullify the concept of divine inspiration. On the contrary, one could argue that it reinforces it.

An early dating of Luke's Gospel makes a meeting between Mary, James and Luke not only possible, but highly likely. Given James' pre-eminent position in the early church,[7] it stands to reason that he would be aware of Luke's intention to write an authoritative gospel account of Jesus life. Luke may in fact, have asked for permission from James and sought his blessing to do so.

We also know that Luke accompanied Paul on his journey to Jerusalem, where together they met with James and the leaders of the church (Acts 21:15–40). Luke would have had an opportunity to discuss and research these matters at that time.

It would also logically follow that both James and Mary would want the events of Jesus annunciation, divine conception, birth and childhood recorded for posterity. Since Mary was already well-advanced in years, this would lend an element of urgency to this project. Full collaboration with Luke is the likely outcome.

Historical records indicate that James died a martyr's death in 64 AD. If Luke's gospel was completed after 64 AD, then James was not the source of the material found in chapters one and two of Luke's gospel. But with each succeeding year, the likelihood of Mary being the eyewitness source also diminishes. This makes an early dating of Luke's gospel eminently plausible.

So, in conclusion, let's return to that moment the boy Jesus said, *"Did you not know that I must be about My Father's business?"* (Luke 2:49 NKJV)

Where was James when Jesus made this declaration? He was likely standing alongside his mother, Mary, and his father, Joseph, as those words were spoken.

Years later, James may also have played a significant role in ensuring that those words were recorded for all generations.

---

[7] For a more thorough discussion of James' leadership role in the early church, see Chapter 12 of this book.

---- 4 ----

The Family Rift

One can easily assume that Jesus, and by extension James, grew up in an idyllic family. If God selected Mary to be the mother of God's own son, then surely, she was a perfect mother—the perfect mother. Joseph too must have been a man of flawless character, a hardworking, salt- of-the-earth fellow with impeccable morals. Growing up in such a home in small-town Nazareth must have been like having your own corner of heaven in this rough and tumble, sin-stained world.

But in this fallen world there is no perfect home and no absolutely perfect family. The taint of sin and the machinations of our ancient foe are everywhere. If it were not so, this world would not need a Savior. It should come as no surprise then, that all was not always sweetness and light in the household of Joseph and Mary. God frequently uses deeply flawed characters.

Luke concludes his account of Jesus' boyhood temple experience with this summary statement:

> Then he [Jesus] went down to Nazareth with them [Mary and Joseph] and was obedient to them. But his mother treasured all these things in her heart. And Jesus grew in wisdom and stature, and in favor with God and man. (Luke 2:51–52)

There is no indication of any family tension in this statement. On the contrary, the opposite appears to be true, and undoubtedly there were many happy moments of family harmony in this home. But when we examine other passages from the four gospel accounts of Jesus life, we can see that below the surface, trouble was brewing within this holy family. How soon family tension and rivalry reared its ugly head remains open to debate, but as we will soon see, it certainly was present during the time of Jesus public ministry.

Sibling rivalry is common among multi-child families. Was there rivalry between Jesus and his brothers as they grew up? Most likely there was. In fact, the very notion of living with a morally perfect, intellectually superior older brother should send shivers of dread through any thinking child. How could any sibling possibly measure up to this older brother's exemplary standard? Here we have the textbook recipe for childhood frustration and sibling resentment.

If Jesus reached an epiphany moment in the temple at age twelve, it is reasonable to surmise that James may have had a similar epiphany in his early teens—a moment when he realized that Jesus was profoundly different, and that unlike himself, Jesus was not the son of Joseph.

This epiphany may have occurred in a rather ordinary way. Teens his own age may have told James that his brother was the son of another man. Small-town communities have a collective memory. Mary's initial unexpected pregnancy likely had tongues wagging. Rumors spread and gain currency with time, and in due time that rumor may have circled round to James.

James did not conclude that Jesus was the Son of God. A more natural explanation was much more logical. It is reasonable to assume that in his judgment, James came to believe that Jesus was the product of his mother's rather unfortunate union with another man. Scripture bears witness to this verdict.

The following passage from John's Gospel provides us with ample evidence of the tension that was rife within this family:

> After this, Jesus went around in Galilee. He did not
> want to go about in Judea because the Jewish leaders

there were looking for a way to kill him. But when the Jewish Festival of Tabernacles was near, Jesus' brothers said to him, "Leave Galilee and go to Judea, so that your disciples there may see the works you do. No one who wants to become a public figure acts in secret. Since you are doing these things, show yourself to the world." For even his own brothers did not believe in him.

Therefore Jesus told them, "My time is not yet here; for you any time will do. The world cannot hate you, but it hates me because I testify that its works are evil. You go to the festival. I am not going up to this festival, because my time has not yet fully come." After he had said this, he stayed in Galilee.

However, after his brothers had left for the festival, he went also, not publicly, but in secret. Now at the festival the Jewish leaders were watching for Jesus and asking, "Where is he?"

Among the crowds there was widespread whispering about him. Some said, "He is a good man."

Others replied, "No, he deceives the people." But no one would say anything publicly about him for fear of the leaders. (John 7:1–13)

John's observation on the brothers' advice is very enlightening. He states, *"For even his brothers did not believe in him."* There was clearly a bitter tension here that the brothers' words alone do not convey. The brothers that this passage refers to are of course James, Joseph, Simon and Judas (Jude), as identified in the Gospel accounts of Matthew, Mark, and Luke.

And what precisely did the brothers not believe about Jesus? From the context, it appears that they *did* believe in his miraculous powers; in fact, they challenged him to reveal himself to the world through them. The phrase that is translated *"the works you do"* in the New International Version is more freely translated *"see your miracles"* in the New Living

Translation. So, it is clear that the brothers had heard the stories of Jesus' miracles or had witnessed them personally. Now they want Jesus to reveal himself to the world. They say, *"Since you are doing these things, show yourself to the world."*

The brothers' unbelief went deeper than a surface acknowledgement of the miracles. They doubted his deity—his divine origin. To his brothers, Jesus was too familiar. He was Mary's boy—their half-brother—nothing more. But beyond that, he was their half-brother, the bastard son, putting on airs, rising above his rightful station in life. Furthermore, they were jealous of his rising popularity as a person of considerable renown.

Here we see the truth of what John said in the introduction to his Gospel, *"He [Jesus] was in the world, and though the world was made through him, the world did not recognize him. He came to that which was his own, but his own did not receive him"* (John 1:10–11).

Jesus was rejected by his own—by his own brothers. They did not recognize him as God or the Son of God.

As one of the three disciples within Jesus' inner circle, John was likely a witness to this conversation between Jesus and his brothers. Now in his Gospel, John bears witness to the brother's unbelief.

But John had another domestic source that may have enlightened him more fully on the brothers' lack of faith. John was responsible for looking after Mary after Jesus' death. Surely the issue of the brothers' early rejection of the messianic Jesus was a topic of discussion at some point.

Undoubtedly, at times Mary would also have encountered the disparaging perspective that her younger sons had toward Jesus. Jesus did not easily fit into a world or even a family that prefers conformity. Those who are struggling to raise exceptional children may find some comfort in that.[8] Often gifted children are misunderstood or not well-received socially by peers and even by adults.[9]

---

[8] Janet L. Jackson explores this concept in her book *Jesus Didn't Fit In: Raising Nontraditional Children* (WestBow, 1993).

[9] For many years I taught a congregated gifted class in a public school setting. Often, despite good social skills, gifted students faced rejection.

Jesus sees through his brothers' advice to their deep-seated antagonism, and consequently he responds harshly to their challenge to reveal himself to the world. But with his response, he provides a clue as to why they rejected him. *"Jesus told them, 'My time is not yet here; for you any time will do.'"*

For the brothers, when they consider Jesus' claims to deity, they see an elephant in the room—perhaps several of them. The largest problem may well be the death of their father Joseph. How could this healer of the sick, this miracle worker, this man who raised the dead to life on more than one occasion do nothing to prevent the death of their father?

The unspoken thought might go something like this, "So Jesus, you're the Son of God! Well, why then did you let Dad die? Why didn't you do something? Why do you go about healing perfect strangers, while your own family suffers?"

But how does Jesus respond? *"Jesus told them, 'My time is not yet here; for you any time will do.'"*

That may be a fine answer for the public, but it does little to soothe an aching heart or comfort the doubting soul of a family member. Why did Jesus raise to life the son of the widow at Nain (Luke 7:11-17), but leave Joseph, his earthly father, to die?

Variations on this question confront us often. Why is one child spared in a school shooting, while others are gunned down by a madman? Why does one woman make a miraculous recovery from terminal cancer, while an equally worthy woman suffers and dies, leaving a grief-stricken family? These questions have no easy answer. None exists on this side of eternity.

Death stalks all of us, and ultimately death always claims its prize. A better question might be, "Why now? Why did this person die now? Why not later?"

"Jesus told them, 'My time is not yet here; for you any time will do.'"

There was no miracle for their father Joseph. Jesus' time had not yet come. His time for doing miracles had not yet arrived. Earlier in John's Gospel, Jesus made a similar pronouncement when Mary asked him to intervene when the wine ran out at the wedding in Cana. *"'Woman, why do you involve me?' Jesus replied. 'My time has not yet come.'"* (John 2:4)

But despite this objection, Jesus proceeded to perform his first miracle as he turned water into wine. The question of timing remains. Why work a miracle in one situation, but not in another? Why heal one invalid at the pool of Bethesda (John 5:1-16), but leave many others to suffer?

Clearly, Jesus was working according to a different timetable. In the present, we tend to think as Jesus' brothers thought. We could always use a miracle or two. For us, when it comes to receiving a miracle, *"any time will do."*

At this point in John's account, there is clearly a great gulf separating these brothers and Jesus, and Jesus does nothing to bridge it. On the contrary he expands the gulf and elaborates on it. Speaking of his brothers, he says, *"The world cannot hate you, but it hates me because I testify that its works are evil. You go to the festival. I am not going up to this festival, because my time has not yet fully come."*

Implied in these remarks is the idea that the brothers are worldly and complicit with the evil of the world. Jesus sees himself as being on a great redemptive mission—a mission set in motion by his heavenly Father. It is a mission of impeccable, precise timing. He will not be distracted, bated or thrown off course by his brothers. For Jesus timing was everything. He will not be hurried into doing miracles or into revealing himself to the world. He will not be hurried to his death in Jerusalem. He is not a showman, a performer or an entertainer for the crowds.

He is a redeemer on a mission—a sacrificial lamb, the Passover lamb—saving himself for slaughter at the right time, the perfect time.

There is a double meaning in the phrase, *"My time is not yet here."* For the brothers it meant the time for Jesus to reveal himself to the world through his miraculous powers, but for Jesus it also meant the time for his approaching death. The Jewish leaders were already plotting his demise. He did not want to speed that day by following his brothers' ill-conceived ideas.

Jesus' brothers understood none of this. They did not believe in him. James did not believe in him. The brothers proceeded to the feast while Jesus stayed for a time in Galilee. The rift between them is clearly defined. They did not travel together. They are walking separate paths.

Jesus has his followers, his disciples, but his brothers are not numbered among them.

Unbelief and a sharp division in the family are not what we would expect from the union of Mary and Joseph. We would like to believe that Mary and Joseph did a stellar job in raising their children; after all they were selected by God for this specific assignment.

But let's be clear: this was no easy task.

Many believe that Mary and Joseph disclosed to Jesus in an age-appropriate manner the divine nature of his origin and the broad outlines of his calling. Surely this was a part of their parental responsibility, a responsibility given to them by God.

Joseph certainly would have trained Jesus in the skills of carpentry. The family would have been active in the local synagogue. A synagogue education would include learning to read and write, but also committing reams of scripture to memory.

This would all be foundational to Jesus' later ministry.

But the parental task of educating Jesus in his messianic calling would be far easier if there were no younger brothers around. Singling out a child for special status or treatment instantly creates family tension. Anyone named Joseph should know this well.

The brothers' rejection of Jesus bears a striking resemblance to another example of sibling rivalry and rejection recorded in the last chapters of Genesis. When he was a teenager, the patriarch Joseph (Joseph of the multicolored coat) was rejected by his brothers. But this was no mild snub. Joseph's brothers initially wanted to kill him, but they settled for selling him to Ishmaelites, who later sold him into slavery in Egypt.[10]

The New Testament Joseph surely must have had his Old Testament namesake in mind as he raised his own family. The parallels run deep. Many biblical scholars have noted that there is a striking similarity between the life of Jesus and the life of Joseph, the patriarch, whose story is recorded in Genesis.

Here in brief are some of these parallels:

---

[10] The account of Joseph's life spans chapters 37–50 of the Book of Genesis.

- Both claimed a special relationship with their father—Jesus' father being God, while Joseph's father was Jacob, who is also called Israel, the father of the nation.[11]
- Both had a revelation of their divine calling at or near puberty.[12]
- Both were rejected by their brothers.[13]
- Though both were tempted, they lived a sinless or exemplary life.[14]
- Both were wrongly accused, arrested and suffered though innocent.[15]
- After suffering both were exalted to rule.[16]
- Both brought deliverance or salvation—Joseph for Egypt, Jesus for the world.[17]
- Both forgave those who wronged them and were reconciled with their brothers.[18]

If the New Testament Joseph showed any special favoritism to Jesus, he risked repeating the mistakes of Jacob, the father of the Joseph of the Old Testament. In that instance, special treatment led directly to fierce resentment and forced exile from the family.

This may have left Joseph in a conundrum. Too much disclosure of Jesus' divine origin and messianic calling put him at risk of resentment and rejection by his siblings. No disclosure at all could be interpreted as a failure of parental responsibility.

Even the meaning of term Messiah is problematic. We understand this word quite differently now. How did Joseph and Mary see their son's

---

[11] Luke 2:49–50; Genesis 37:3–4.

[12] Luke 2:41–52; Genesis 37:5–11.

[13] John 1:11 and John 7:5; Genesis 37:12–32.

[14] Matthew 4:11 and 2 Corinthians 5:21; Genesis 39:6–15.

[15] Mark 14:43–15:41; Genesis 39:19–21.

[16] Philippians 2:9–11; Genesis 41:41–44.

[17] John 3:16; Genesis 50:20.

[18] Luke 23:34; Genesis 50:21.

calling? They were looking at him through first century Jewish eyes, and they likely had expectations and perspectives that were quite different from ours today.

The desire for a Jewish Messiah to arise from among the people was pervasive during this historic period. The felt need was for a strong leader to arise and rally the people, so they could overthrow the oppressive pagan rule of Rome by means of a bloody insurrection. From the Jewish perspective the need and the vision were clear. This Messiah—the anointed one—would re-establish the throne of David and with a rod of iron he would rule over Israel and the surrounding nations in righteousness and justice.

The firstborn son in Joseph's household had the right lineage. He was a son of David and furthermore, at his birth his messianic call was confirmed by the words of angels, prophets and magi. Surely at the right time Joseph would or should instill into Jesus the imperatives of his messianic call. Did Joseph do this?

On this topic the scriptures are maddeningly silent. Joseph dies at some point between Jesus' boyhood visit to the temple and the emergence of his public ministry. When or how is unknown.

If Joseph and Mary followed the wisdom of the day, they would have imparted an incorrect messianic vision. Several would-be messiahs rose up in rebellion against Rome before and after Jesus' crucifixion. Each rebellion was brutally crushed until the Jews were finally expelled from Jerusalem and their homeland in 135 AD.

The rebellion that Jesus would eventually lead was a soft power rebellion that rejected bloodshed and the use of force.[19] But ultimately the kingdom of God, which Jesus founded, would triumph over the empire of Rome. Down through the ages to the present day, his followers have submitted to his rule within a kingdom that never ends.

In matters affecting family dynamics, timing is crucial. In the right time, the dreams of the Joseph of the technicolor coat would come true. His parents and brothers would bow down to him. Joseph, the son of Israel, became the ruler of all of Egypt.

---

[19] *Jesus said, 'My kingdom is not of this world. If it were, my servants would fight to prevent my arrest by the Jewish leaders. But now my kingdom is from another place.'* (John 18:36).

In the right time, Jesus' brothers beginning with James would recognize him as the Son of God and the Savior of the world. They too would bow before him as king. All would come in the right time, including reconciliation.

Prior to the disagreement with his unbelieving brothers cited in John 7, Jesus was in conflict with the Jewish leadership in Judea. This too was a conflict over timing. He had dared to heal a man on the Sabbath.[20] In his discourse with the Jewish leadership, Jesus gives us a glimpse into his modus operandi:

> Very truly I tell you, the Son can do nothing by himself; he can do only what he sees his Father doing, because whatever the Father does the Son also does. For the Father loves the Son and shows him all he does. Yes, and he will show him even greater works than these, so that you will be amazed. For just as the Father raises the dead and gives them life, even so the Son gives life to whom he is pleased to give it. Moreover, the Father judges no one, but has entrusted all judgment to the Son, that all may honor the Son just as they honor the Father. Whoever does not honor the Son does not honor the Father, who sent him. (John 5:19–23)

These words leave no doubt about whose agenda Jesus is following. He is going about his Father's business. The twelve-year-old has grown up. Joseph is dead. The thirty-year-old Jesus is moving according to the dictates of his heavenly Father. He does *only what he sees his Father doing.*

Without doubt, what Jesus does, he does in his Father's perfect timing. As we shall see, pursuing his messianic call would bring him into direct conflict with his brother—James the unbeliever.

---

[20] In Jerusalem at the Pool of Bethesda, Jesus healed a disabled man on the Sabbath. He exacerbated this perceived infraction of the Sabbath law by telling the man to roll up his sleeping mat and go home. A full description of this miraculous healing and the ensuing debate with Jewish authorities can be found in fifth chapter of John's gospel.

Did Joseph and Mary fail in their parental mandate because we see evidence of serious conflict and unbelief within their family? If these saintly parents were unable to raise their family in harmony and faith, what hope do Christian parents have today?

Concluding that Joseph and Mary somehow failed in their parental mandate is unwarranted. Right actions stemming from right motives are often misunderstood, particularly within the dynamics of a large and growing family. Children, particularly adult children, are accountable for their own attitudes and actions.

In some respects, the Genesis account of Joseph's life serves as a template for what unfolds 1,500 years later in the family of Mary and Joseph. Division and conflict bubble to the surface, but ultimately all is resolved through salvation and forgiveness.

Interestingly, the Book of Genesis ends with this statement:

> So Joseph died at the age of a hundred and ten. And after they embalmed him, he was placed in a coffin in Egypt. (Genesis 50:26)

Four hundred years later, after a great deliverance, the stone box containing Joseph's bones was carried out of Egypt and into the land of Israel. There his bones found their ultimate resting place.

> And Joseph's bones, which the Israelites had brought up from Egypt, were buried at Shechem in the tract of land that Jacob bought for a hundred pieces of silver from the sons of Hamor, the father of Shechem. This became the inheritance of Joseph's descendants. (Joshua 24:32)

Two thousand years after the death of the New Testament Joseph, we encounter another stone burial box. In the Hebrew language it bears this inscription: "James, son of Joseph, brother of Jesus."

 5

A House Divided

The family rift that is evident in John's Gospel did not appear overnight. Undoubtedly, it had been growing for years. Most likely it worsened after Joseph's death. His authority as the head of the home would certainly have had a calming effect, but with his passing, the simmering rivalry between the sons of Joseph and the firstborn son of Mary boiled to the surface.

Luke tells us that Jesus was thirty years old when he began his public ministry (Luke 3:23). All four gospel writers agree that it was his relative, John the Baptist, who lit the spark in Jesus that set the world ablaze. [21] Jesus' baptism by his cousin John was the starting point of the meteoric rise of Jesus' ministry (Luke 1:36). The latent potential of his divine DNA suddenly came alive. His baptism experience marked a dramatic turning point in his life.

> When all the people were being baptized, Jesus was baptized too. And as he was praying, heaven was opened and the Holy Spirit descended on him in bodily form like a dove. And a voice came from heaven: "You are my Son, whom I love; with you I am well pleased." (Luke 3:21–22)

---

[21] Luke 1:36, Matthew 3:13–14, Mark 1:4-8, John 1:29–31.

The three synoptic gospels, Matthew, Mark and Luke provide essentially the same description of this transformative event. The Triune God is manifest: Father, Son and Holy Spirit. The Father speaks words of affirmation to his Son, and the Holy Spirit descends in bodily form to empower Jesus for the mission that lay before him. The gospel writers leave no doubt that everything that follows in Jesus' ministry had its starting point in this turning-point experience.

If Jesus the man ever questioned his own divinity, every shred of doubt was removed in that moment. This was heaven-sent confirmation. His Father had spoken—had spoken audibly. From the age of twelve, Jesus knew of his divine origin—his life source—and now he knew his destiny. He was God's son. Though his brothers rejected him, though the world rejected him, he knew the love of his Father. And in the days that followed, nothing would deflect him from doing his Father's will.

Called, chosen and approved by his Father, Jesus was now ready to walk out his redemptive mission.

John the Evangelist, the gospel writer, gives us a different perspective on this event. In John's gospel we see the baptism of Jesus through the eyes of the one who performed it, John the Baptist:

> The next day John saw Jesus coming toward him and said, "Look, the Lamb of God, who takes away the sin of the world! This is the one I meant when I said, 'A man who comes after me has surpassed me because he was before me.' I myself did not know him, but the reason I came baptizing with water was that he might be revealed to Israel."
>
> Then John gave this testimony: "I saw the Spirit come down from heaven as a dove and remain on him. And I myself did not know him, but the one who sent me to baptize with water told me, 'The man on whom you see the Spirit come down and remain is the one who will baptize with the Holy Spirit.' I have seen and I testify that this is God's Chosen One." (John 1:29–34)

John the Baptist's testimony adds considerably to our understanding of this life-defining event. Chiefly, he identifies for us who Jesus really is. In a moment of divine revelation, he declares, *"Look, the Lamb of God, who takes away the sin of the world!"*

John the Baptist did not live to witness Jesus' death on the cross, but in that instant, he caught a glimpse of what lay ahead for the man he identified as the Messiah. He saw the sacrificial nature of Jesus' mission.

In his own words, John tells us his own mission has now been fulfilled. *"The reason I came baptizing with water was that he might be revealed to Israel."*

John the Baptist's ministry will decrease; the ministry of the Christ, the anointed one, will increase. The torch has been passed. The new covenant has begun.

The Baptist makes no mention of the Father's affirming voice from heaven, but he provides more detail about the coming of the Holy Spirit. He emphasizes that the Spirit remained on Jesus. From that moment on, the miraculous power that is evident in Jesus' life can be directly attributed to the Holy Spirit remaining on him.

John's endorsement of Jesus' divine calling and ministry stand in sharp contrast to the rejection Jesus would later experience from James and the other members of his immediate family. For reasons we will never fully know, this blood relative recognized in Jesus what his brothers completely missed. Those who are too close sometimes fail to grasp what is patently evident to an outsider. Undoubtedly, John's affirmation of Jesus carried considerable weight, since he was a public figure of national renown. Yet as we will see, it did not appear to persuade James.

This raises the question of where James stood regarding John the Baptist. There is no indication in scripture that James and the other family members submitted to John's baptism. The gospel writers and John in particular give us the impression that Jesus acted alone. He came for baptism apart from his family. This was solely his decision, without the support or presence of his family.

This seems rather unusual given that John the Baptist was a close relative, and there was a strong bond between Mary and John's mother Elizabeth at the time of their pregnancies—a bond so strong that

Mary spent three months living in the home of Zechariah and Elizabeth (Luke 1:39–56). Though the gospels are silent on this matter, it is easy to imagine these two families spending time with each other on special occasions such as the Passover. It is not unreasonable to surmise that as boys, John, Jesus, and James were playmates. Did they drift apart over time or was there a sudden rupture in relations?

In his adult life did James disapprove of John the Baptist's message and tactics? The gospels leave the impression that John's call for repentance and baptism was broadly accepted by the people of the time, but he raised the ire of one particular group.

> But when he [John] saw many of the Pharisees and Sadducees coming to where he was baptizing, he said to them: "You brood of vipers! Who warned you to flee from the coming wrath? Produce fruit in keeping with repentance. And do not think you can say to yourselves, 'We have Abraham as our father.' I tell you that out of these stones God can raise up children for Abraham." (Matthew 3:7–9)

Later in Jesus' interaction with the Pharisees and religious authorities, it is abundantly clear that they have rejected John's call for repentance.[22] If James embraced the teachings of the Pharisees, it is probable that he opposed John's message and his call for baptism. With their strict adherence to the Law and their extreme pride in Jewish heritage, the Pharisees and their teachings might have found a welcome home within the mind of James. His writings have often been described as having a legalistic bent.

If as a young man James fell under the sway of the Pharisees, he would find himself opposing both John the Baptist and Jesus, his own brother. Again, though the scriptures are silent on this topic, it seems quite likely that this was a family divided along religious lines.

The writers of the synoptic Gospels tell us that immediately following his baptism, Jesus entered a forty-day period of fasting:

---

[22] See Matthew 21:23–27.

> At once the Spirit sent him out into the wilderness, and he was in the wilderness forty days, being tempted by Satan. He was with the wild animals, and angels attended him. (Mark 1:12–13)

Then, having overcome the temptations of the flesh and of Satan,[23] Jesus began his public ministry in the power of the Holy Spirit and under the watchful eye of his heavenly Father. The impact across the region is felt almost immediately.

Matthew gives us this summative overview:

> Jesus went throughout Galilee, teaching in their synagogues, proclaiming the good news of the kingdom, and healing every disease and sickness among the people. News about him spread all over Syria, and people brought to him all who were ill with various diseases, those suffering severe pain, the demon-possessed, those having seizures, and the paralyzed; and he healed them. Large crowds from Galilee, the Decapolis, Jerusalem, Judea and the region across the Jordan followed him. (Matthew 4:23–25)

What had come over the carpenter's son? What did Jesus' family think of this dramatic turn of events? Within a few months this young man, conceived out of wedlock, had become a much sought after religious teacher, a healer, and a crowd-gathering celebrity. Did they approve?

Mark's Gospel provides us with a clear answer:

> Then Jesus entered a house, and again a crowd gathered, so that he and his disciples were not even able to eat. When his family heard about this, they went to take charge of him, for they said, "He is out of his mind." (Mark 3:20–21)

---

[23] For a full account of Christ's temptation in the desert see Matthew 4:1–11.

The answer is an unambiguous "No!" No, they did not approve. They thought he was insane. We know from John's Gospel that Jesus' brothers did not believe in him. Now we discover that they truly thought he had gone mad. Their own words best convey their rendered judgement, "He is out of his mind."

They considered him to be a raving lunatic incapable of conducting his own affairs. Why else would they go to take charge of him? Furthermore, they were not alone in this opinion. Mark's account continues:

> And the teachers of the law who came down from Jerusalem said, "He is possessed by Beelzebul! By the prince of demons he is driving out demons."
>
> So Jesus called them over to him and began to speak to them in parables: "How can Satan drive out Satan? If a kingdom is divided against itself, that kingdom cannot stand. If a house is divided against itself, that house cannot stand. And if Satan opposes himself and is divided, he cannot stand; his end has come. In fact, no one can enter a strong man's house without first tying him up. Then he can plunder the strong man's house. Truly I tell you, people can be forgiven all their sins and every slander they utter, but whoever blasphemes against the Holy Spirit will never be forgiven; they are guilty of an eternal sin."
>
> He said this because they were saying, "He has an impure spirit." (Mark 3:22–30)

In brief, Jesus' family thought he was insane and the teachers of the law from Jerusalem thought he was demon possessed. The opinion of these teachers of the law may have had a good deal of influence on James. It is worth noting that these would be the same religious leaders from Judea that according to John were trying to kill Jesus.[24] This can hardly be described as a resounding endorsement of Jesus' ministry!

---

[24] See John 7:1.

But then Jesus has always been a controversial figure throughout history. The great twentieth-century thinker C.S. Lewis, in his defense of orthodox Christian faith, makes this insightful statement regarding Jesus:

> I am trying here to prevent anyone saying the really foolish thing that people often say about Him: I'm ready to accept Jesus as a great moral teacher, but I don't accept his claim to be God. That is the one thing we must not say. A man who was merely a man and said the sort of things Jesus said would not be a great moral teacher. He would either be a lunatic—on the level with the man who says he is a poached egg—or else he would be the Devil of Hell. You must make your choice. Either this man was, and is, the Son of God, or else a madman or something worse. You can shut him up for a fool, you can spit at him and kill him as a demon or you can fall at his feet and call him Lord and God, but let us not come with any patronizing nonsense about his being a great human teacher. He has not left that open to us. He did not intend to.[25]

There is no convenient middle ground concerning Jesus. It has always been thus, even for the members of his immediate family. Yet there is one thing abundantly clear from Mark's account: this is a deeply divided family. Mary may have believed in the messianic mission of her firstborn son, but it is apparent her other sons do not. They believe Jesus is out of his mind, and, bringing their mother with them, they set off to rescue their errant half-brother from his delusion.

In his discussion with the teachers of the law, Jesus refutes the idea that he is demon possessed with the argument that a kingdom or a house divided against itself cannot stand. There is a good deal of irony at play here since his own family is divided, and now he finds himself on the outs with most of them. Do they too believe he is demon possessed? Quite possibly, though we are not explicitly told.

---

[25] C.S. Lewis, *Mere Christianity* (MacMillan, 1952), pp. 55–56.

Mark continues his account of these events:

> Then Jesus' mother and brothers arrived. Standing outside, they sent someone in to call him. A crowd was sitting around him, and they told him, "Your mother and brothers are outside looking for you."
>
> "Who are my mother and my brothers?" he asked.
>
> Then he looked at those seated in a circle around him and said, "Here are my mother and my brothers! Whoever does God's will is my brother and sister and mother." (Mark 3:31–35)

Obedient Christian believers—Christ's followers—draw a great deal of warmth and comfort from this passage. They are identified as brothers, sisters, and mothers to their Lord. What amazing words of love and embrace!

But there is a stinging flip side to this affirmation. The members of Jesus' own family stand excluded. Both literally and figuratively they are on the outside—on the outside of the home looking in. For them this is a backhanded rebuke of the highest magnitude. They are not deemed to be part of this happy family of followers—Jesus' spiritual family—but neither do they want to be.

What appears to follow (though Mark provides us with no further details) is a classic standoff. We are not even told if Jesus agrees to go out and meet with his biological family; presumably he did not. If he knew their intentions, it may have been wise to not meet with them. The brothers might try to take him by force.

Were harsh words exchanged? Perhaps.

Did Jesus try to reassure them that he was sound of mind? Maybe. The silence of scripture on this matter allows some room for conjecture.

But ultimately from the three gospel accounts that record this incident,[26] we can only reach one conclusion: Jesus continues on with his ministry, and his brothers returned to Nazareth without their wayward older sibling. They may consider him insane, but Jesus is not about to

---

[26] Matthew 12:46–50, Mark 3:31–35, Luke 8:19–21.

change course and yield to their will. He is doing his Father's will. He is going about his Father's business.

The rift between them has widened immeasurably. Can it ever be bridged? In effect Jesus has disowned them, and they in turn have abandoned him to his own will. The gulf between them is enormous.

In the days ahead the implications of this rift will play out in stunning ways.

—— 6 ——

The Role of James

The dominant role that James played in the development of the rift between Jesus and the other members of the family should not be underestimated. With the death of Joseph, Jesus should have become the *de facto* head of the family. Being the firstborn son held great significance in the Jewish culture of that time, and with it came a number of responsibilities and privileges. The role of chief provider and final authority in family matters was certainly part of the package. Some of these responsibilities were cultural expectations, but others were actual requirements in the oral tradition, which later became Talmudic law.

Now here is the unenviable position that Jesus finds himself in. He is the firstborn, but he is not the son of Joseph. To use the colloquial term, he is the bastard son of another man—or so it would seem. Certainly, this is how the community would likely see him.

In a tight-knit, semi-rural community, it is reasonable to believe that from the moment of Mary's initial pregnancy, there were whispers and hints of juicy gossip. Mary and Joseph were not living together. How did she get pregnant? Was this baby really Joseph's son? As the child grew, in all likelihood it became evident from Jesus' appearance that he was not Joseph's boy. The local wags probably had great sport debating who the real father was.

To the natural mind, Mary's tale of the visit from the angel Gabriel and conception by the Holy Spirit makes little logical sense. It is highly unlikely that she repeated this story to anyone except Joseph and perhaps her parents. Why say anything to anyone else? Why invite open ridicule from other family members, her friends and her neighbours? Let them think what they will. She knew the secret of Jesus conception: a secret it would remain. From Luke's account of the lost boy Jesus in the temple courts, it is apparent that she did not even tell her son of his divine origin. It was left up to him to discover the identity of his true Father.

As for James and his younger brothers, as discussed earlier, they either discerned independently that Jesus was somehow different—not fully one of them—or they heard it from their neighbours and friends. They even may have heard it from Jesus himself. He was not shy in identifying himself as God's son in the temple courts at age twelve. It is possible that young James and his brothers overheard Jesus' response to his parents at that time, though they may not have originally understood the meaning and implications of his words. He may also have spoken with them about the identity of his real Father on other occasions, occasions not recorded in scripture, just as the patriarch Joseph revealed his divine destiny to his incredulous brothers (Genesis 37:5–11).

Finally, Jesus' keen intellect, his love for the sacred scriptures and his general conduct surely set him apart from the other teens and young men in Nazareth. However, being different does not necessarily correspond with being accepted or popular among your peers. As pointed out earlier, Jesus' ministry at the local synagogue was greeted with skepticism and open hostility by the townspeople (Mark 6:1–6, Luke 4:16–30.). Additionally, his brothers did not believe in him. Though Jesus attracted many followers, many disciples—other young men like themselves—not one of his younger brothers are numbered among the apostolic band. As we have already witnessed, the relationship between them was tense and poisoned.

Without question, the death of Joseph must have raised several thorny issues. Did James recognize Jesus as the new head of the home? If Jesus was not the son of Joseph, then the privileges and responsibilities of headship should legitimately fall to James, Joseph's firstborn—not to Jesus. For this reason, did the local religious community recognize James in the leadership role? Or did they recognize Jesus as the head of the household? Authorities in the local synagogue may well have had a say in this matter.

Primogeniture also affected the family inheritance. Who was rightfully the firstborn in this case? And what role, if any, did Mary play in all this? Was she simply a bystander while the male members of the family and the synagogue rulers sorted out these matters?

Though Jesus' half-brothers did not believe in him, without a doubt his mother did. She knew and experienced the miraculous nature of his conception and birth. She marvelled at the prophetic words spoken over Jesus at his dedication in the temple (Luke 2:22–38). We are told that *"Mary treasured up all these things and pondered them in her heart"* (Luke 2:19). In addition, her words of concern prompted Jesus to perform the first miracle of his public ministry, as he turned water into wine (John 2:1–11). It is abundantly clear from the gospel accounts that Mary believed in the divinity of her firstborn. Undoubtedly, after the death of her husband, she found herself caught in the middle between her two strong-willed sons, Jesus and James.

To the present-day postmodern, the issue of primogeniture may seem to be socially insignificant, but this was of great significance to the society of this period. Even if there were strong amicable relations between these two brothers, this would still be a very trying question. If there existed the slightest hint of rivalry, unresolved grievances, or a competitive spirit, these issues could quickly turn into strife and bitter malice. It is reasonable to speculate that they did.

The Bible is largely silent on these matters. We have no indication as to when or how Joseph died. We catch only a few glimpses of the dynamics among the now full-grown members of the family, but the picture that emerges is rather disturbing. During the time of Jesus' ministry, this appears to have been a household that is dysfunctional and deeply divided.

Did Jesus even want to be recognized as the head of Joseph's home? Perhaps it was a responsibility that fell to him, but he did not want to bear it, since, according to his genetic code, he knew it was a role that was not rightfully his. Perhaps he took on the headship role through a sense of duty, but at every turn he faced resistance and resentment from his half-brothers.

James the oldest son of Joseph would have led this resistance, and an ambitious James may have been willing and eager to usurp Jesus' authority. After all, he saw the leadership role as lawfully his. There were ample grounds for rancorous contention in this family, and by stitching together what we can discern from the gospel accounts, division and tension were clearly present as outlined below:

- When Jesus left the family home to be baptized by John, his departure may have served partially as an escape from a poisoned home environment. Forty days of fasting in the desert may have been preferable to the ongoing rancour in Nazareth.
- This much we can ascertain from the gospel accounts: by the time of the rupture in family relations recorded in Mark 3:20–35, James is firmly in charge of the household.
- As the eldest son of Joseph, he is chief among the brotherhood of unbelievers that make up his family as recorded in John 7:1–13.
- In consultation with his brothers, he has determined that Jesus *"Is out of his mind"* (Mark 3: 21).
- He has organized a family expedition to take charge of his deranged half-brother.
- Despite his best efforts, he has failed to make Jesus see the error of his ways or regain control of what he likely sees as a dangerous and irrational member of his household (Mark 3:31-35).

The half-brothers part ways. In the synoptic gospels this is their last recorded meeting before Jesus' death.

For Jesus this rupture in relations means liberty. He is no longer answerable to James for his life and conduct. He is accountable only to God. From the time of his baptism by John, Jesus has extricated himself from the oppressive confines of his brother's household. He is no longer the carpenter's son. He has discovered his true identity as the Son of God, and now at age thirty, for the first time in his life, he is able to freely walk out the full meaning of that identity.

In the same way, Jesus called on his disciples to abandon all, including family, and come and follow him in a radical new way of life.[27]

He is the Son of God. This truth becomes the central theme—the very core—of his teaching. His followers are children of God. He teaches them to pray to their heavenly Father. The fatherhood of God is at the heart of his message to the people. In the gospels, Jesus only directly addresses God by the name of 'father' or even '*abba*' (daddy) except when quoting scripture.

As cited earlier, when he is called to see his mother and brothers outside the home where he is teaching, he answered,

> "Who are my mother and my brothers?"
> Then he looked at those seated in a circle around him and said, "Here are my mother and my brothers! Whoever does God's will is my brother and sister and mother." (Mark 3:31–35)

Please note Jesus does not say, "Whoever does God's will is my brother and sister and mother *and father.*"

The father figure appears to be missing in this happy family circle. Or is he? For Jesus, his father is God, and his heavenly Father oversees this—his spiritual family gathered before him. His followers are his family.

The fatherhood of God is so central to Jesus that he later instructs his disciples with these words:

> But you are not to be called 'Rabbi,' for you have one Teacher, and you are all brothers. And do not call

---

[27] *Large crowds were traveling with Jesus, and turning to them he said: "If anyone comes to me and does not hate father and mother, wife and children, brothers and sisters—yes, even their own life—such a person cannot be my disciple. And whoever does not carry their cross and follow me cannot be my disciple.* (Luke 14:25–27)

anyone on earth 'father,' for you have one Father, and he is in heaven. Nor are you to be called instructors, for you have one Instructor, the Messiah. (Matthew 23:8–10)

Indeed, according to Jesus' radical new teaching, entrance into the kingdom of God is only possible through spiritual rebirth. Natural birth is insufficient. God must become your Father through the inner working of the Holy Spirit. His conversation with the Pharisee Nicodemus makes this point clear:

He came to Jesus at night and said, "Rabbi, we know that you are a teacher who has come from God. For no one could perform the signs you are doing if God were not with him."

Jesus replied, "Very truly I tell you, no one can see the kingdom of God unless they are born again."

"How can someone be born when they are old?" Nicodemus asked. "Surely they cannot enter a second time into their mother's womb to be born!"

Jesus answered, "Very truly I tell you, no one can enter the kingdom of God unless they are born of water and the Spirit. Flesh gives birth to flesh, but the Spirit gives birth to spirit. You should not be surprised at my saying, 'You must be born again.'" (John 3:2–7)

Citizenship in the heavenly kingdom is only conferred on those who are born of the Spirit through faith. Jesus made his own conception by the Holy Spirit the blueprint for his followers. They too must become living repositories of divine DNA. They too, by the process of spiritual rebirth, must become children of the heavenly Father. Baptism by immersion came to symbolize this inner transformation—this spiritual rebirth.

In his introductory remarks on the ministry of Jesus, John gives us further insight into this new creation—this new birth into the family of God:

> He [Jesus] came to that which was his own, but his own
> did not receive him. Yet to all who did receive him, to
> those who believed in his name, he gave the right to
> become children of God—children born not of natural
> descent, nor of human decision or a husband's will, but
> born of God. (John 1:11–13)

Though Jesus was rejected by members of his own family as insane, he started a new spiritual family, a family born of God. Within that spiritual family he found a love and acceptance that superseded that of his brothers and sisters by birth. The importance of family by natural descent was replaced by the importance of spiritual rebirth. This was a radically new family—God's family.

We can easily underestimate the dramatic shift in thinking that this required of his followers. Approaching God as a loving Father was a truly revolutionary concept. The Jewish God was austere, stern, distant and demanding; or so it was thought. But Jesus, God's son, presented a totally different view of Him. He saw a caring Father who was as close as a whispered prayer—as near as our next breath. In the Old Testament the dominant metaphor for God is king—the ultimate ruler; in the gospels it is father—a family member.

Jesus' Sermon on the Mount presents us with a compassionate God who truly cares about his people:

> Look at the birds of the air; they do not sow or reap
> or store away in barns, and yet your heavenly Father
> feeds them. Are you not much more valuable than
> they? Can any one of you by worrying add a single
> hour to your life?
>
> And why do you worry about clothes? See how the
> flowers of the field grow. They do not labor or spin. Yet
> I tell you that not even Solomon in all his splendor was
> dressed like one of these. If that is how God clothes
> the grass of the field, which is here today and tomor-
> row is thrown into the fire, will he not much more

clothe you—you of little faith? So do not worry, saying, 'What shall we eat?' or 'What shall we drink?' or
'What shall we wear?' For the pagans run after all these
things, and your heavenly Father knows that you need
them. But seek first his kingdom and his righteousness,
and all these things will be given to you as well. Therefore do not worry about tomorrow, for tomorrow will
worry about itself. Each day has enough trouble of its
own. (Matthew 6:26–34)

The contemporary teachers of the law were all about the outward
observance of the rules and strict adherence to the rigours of the written code. This was a tightly controlled and religiously regimented society. In this stifling social atmosphere, the message that Jesus brought
was like a breath of fresh air. God was not an uptight, omniscient slave
master. He was actually a loving heavenly Father, who provided for his
children's needs.

It should come as no surprise then that people flocked to his teaching.

The implications of spiritual rebirth—this born-again experience—
cannot be overstated. In a society where the family unit was all-import-
ant, this was a dramatic departure from the norm. The Jewish faith was
and is rooted in the family from its very inception, beginning with the
family of Abraham. Your place within the faith is based on heredity and
lineage. You are a Jew because you were born a Jew—because your parents are Jewish, you can trace back your lineage to Abraham.

Furthermore, this is a closed tribal system. Entrance into the faith,
with very few exceptions, is exclusively by birth. God's chosen people are
chosen by birth. According to accepted Jewish teaching of the time, God
has no adopted children. You must be born into the faith. Jews saw (and
continue to see) themselves as heirs to the covenant God made first with
Abraham, then with Moses, and then the children of Israel. But Jesus
was describing a new, more direct way of relating to God.

The only way for a male outsider to enter this closed religious system was by a dramatic, painful and even dangerous outward physical

change—circumcision. A woman's only portal into the faith was through her husband or father.

Jesus' teaching on entrance into the kingdom of God through spiritual rebirth threw this entire religious system into disarray. It began with the repentance call of John the Baptist:

> John said to the crowds coming out to be baptized by him, "You brood of vipers! Who warned you to flee from the coming wrath? Produce fruit in keeping with repentance. And do not begin to say to yourselves, 'We have Abraham as our father.' For I tell you that out of these stones God can raise up children for Abraham. The ax is already at the root of the trees, and every tree that does not produce good fruit will be cut down and thrown into the fire." (Luke 3:7–9)

The Jewish leadership rejected John's message of repentance and baptism even as they later rejected the message of rebirth as preached by Jesus. They needed no repentance; they were children of Abraham. Their lineage alone guaranteed them a place in the kingdom of God, or so they thought. Jesus did not hesitate to prick their self-righteous balloon:

> To the Jews who had believed him, Jesus said, "If you hold to my teaching, you are really my disciples. Then you will know the truth, and the truth will set you free."
>
> They answered him, "We are Abraham's descendants and have never been slaves of anyone. How can you say that we shall be set free?"
>
> Jesus replied, "Very truly I tell you, everyone who sins is a slave to sin. Now a slave has no permanent place in the family, but a son belongs to it forever. So if the Son sets you free, you will be free indeed. I know that you are Abraham's descendants. Yet you are looking for a way to kill me, because you have no room for

my word. I am telling you what I have seen in the Father's presence, and you are doing what you have heard from your father."

"Abraham is our father," they answered.

"If you were Abraham's children," said Jesus, "then you would do what Abraham did. As it is, you are looking for a way to kill me, a man who has told you the truth that I heard from God. Abraham did not do such things. You are doing the works of your own father."

"We are not illegitimate children," they protested. "The only Father we have is God himself."

Jesus said to them, "If God were your Father, you would love me, for I have come here from God. I have not come on my own; God sent me. Why is my language not clear to you? Because you are unable to hear what I say. You belong to your father, the devil, and you want to carry out your father's desires. He was a murderer from the beginning, not holding to the truth, for there is no truth in him. When he lies, he speaks his native language, for he is a liar and the father of lies. Yet because I tell the truth, you do not believe me! Can any of you prove me guilty of sin? If I am telling the truth, why don't you believe me? Whoever belongs to God hears what God says. The reason you do not hear is that you do not belong to God." (John 8:31–47)

Jesus looked beyond the outward and physical into the heart.[28] The human heart needs to be cleansed through repentance, and the human spirit, dead in sin, needs to be born again by faith through the Holy Spirit. This teaching was completely contrary to the outward religious standard of the times. For many, religion was merely an ongoing parade of hypocrisy. It was a public show one engaged in for the sake of appearance, but Jesus continually cut through the religious clutter to get to the

---

[28] See Matthew 15:10–20.

heart. In his sermon on the mount, Jesus pointed out this hypocrisy and called for a genuine change of heart.[29]

Furthermore, Jesus allowed no place for middle ground. You align yourself either for or against him. In that respect he was and is a highly divisive figure. In the discourse cited above, Jesus essentially called his detractors sons of the devil. They in turn thought the same of him:

> The Jews answered him, "Aren't we right in saying that you are a Samaritan and demon-possessed?" (John 8:48)

This was an insult of the highest order, but Jesus did not back down. In fact, he upped the ante. He closed off this heated discussion in the temple courts by claiming to be God:

> "Very truly I tell you," Jesus answered, "before Abraham was born, I am!" At this, they picked up stones to stone him, but Jesus hid himself, slipping away from the temple grounds. (John 8:58–59)

He did not say, "Before Abraham was born, I was." Jesus said, "*Before Abraham was born, I am.*" In so doing, he identified himself as Deity, the pre-existent one, the creator of the universe and the great "I am" of the Hebrew covenant.[30]

To his listeners, this was blasphemy of the highest order. One should not be surprised that they tried to stone him. These are not the words of someone whom society would consider normal. They resembled the ravings of a madman.

So, then it would appear that James was right. His older brother was "*out of his mind*" (Mark 4:21). Here in Jesus' own words, we have the text that proves that James was right in trying to prevent his brother from propagating this lunacy—this heresy—this fanatical teaching. Jesus claimed to be God. There can be no doubt that James believed

---

[29] See Matthew 6:1–18.

[30] See Exodus 3:14.

Jesus would bring disgrace upon the whole family. This is why James distanced himself from his older brother. Undoubtedly, James also used his influence to prevent the other family members from falling under the spell of his brother, the deluded heretic.

As for Jesus, having left his natural family, he founded his own spiritual family of followers. From these he demanded absolute personal loyalty:

> Do not suppose that I have come to bring peace to the earth. I did not come to bring peace, but a sword. For I have come to turn
>> 'a man against his father, a daughter against her mother,
>> a daughter-in-law against her mother-in-law—a man's enemies will be the members of his own household.'
>
> Anyone who loves their father or mother more than me is not worthy of me; anyone who loves their son or daughter more than me is not worthy of me. Whoever does not take up their cross and follow me is not worthy of me. Whoever finds their life will lose it, and whoever loses their life for my sake will find it. (Matthew 10:34–39)

Membership in Jesus' family of born-again believers required absolute commitment—a commitment that superseded one's commitment to flesh and blood family members. The cost of true discipleship was high, and it remains high today.

But Jesus was not asking his disciples to do anything that he did not ask of himself. His own household was divided and hostile to his mission. In a very real sense, his statement simply reflects the strife and division Jesus experienced within his family. He faced extreme opposition from his own family, and he anticipated that his disciples would face the same level of hostility as they chose to wholeheartedly follow him. Many believers throughout history and even today face severe opposition from family members as they seek to follow Jesus. Some have paid the ultimate price as martyrs at the hands of enraged family members.

Yes, Jesus came to bring a sword. He divided the Jewish nation, and he divided his family. The number of his followers—his spiritual family—was growing, but so too was the opposition to his ministry.

Soon Mary would feel the soul-piercing power of the sword. This was the sword that the prophet Simeon spoke of during Jesus' dedication as an infant in the temple many years earlier.

> Then Simeon blessed them and said to Mary, his mother: "This child is destined to cause the falling and rising of many in Israel, and to be a sign that will be spoken against, so that the thoughts of many hearts will be revealed. And a sword will pierce your own soul too." (Luke 2:34)

—— 7 ——

The Final Cut

At this point many readers may feel that this rift in Jesus' natural family is overstated. Theologians and Bible scholars generally have not raised this matter, and it certainly is not a point of common discussion among believers, or a Sunday sermon topic within churches today. However, when one takes the time to connect the dots—make the links—the biblical record is quite clear. Jesus came from a dysfunctional family. A massive family rift existed between Jesus and his half-brothers, and James was at the crux of this division. No event brings this out more clearly than the crucifixion of Jesus.

But before we connect that final dot, let's review the evidence of this rift as it has been presented thus far:

- Jesus was rejected by the people of his hometown, Nazareth, and barely escaped being thrown off the cliff on which the town was built.[31]
- According to John, the gospel writer, Jesus' brothers did not believe in him or his divine mission.[32]
- At a point early in Jesus' three-year ministry, his brothers and his mother came to get Jesus because they believed he was out

---

[31] Luke 4:16–30; see also Matthew 13:54–58 and Mark 6:1–6.

[32] See John 7:1–13.

of his mind. In response, Jesus identified his followers as his true family.[33] Jesus taught a counter-cultural gospel of spiritual rebirth into God's family.[34]

- Membership in this new spiritual family required a radical loyalty to Christ, which superseded the importance of one's blood relatives.[35]

The picture that emerges is quite clear. Following his baptism by John, Jesus left home and assumed a new identity—his true identity. He no longer identifies as the son of Joseph. He is the Son of God, even as the voice coming from heaven identified him at his baptism.[36] His birth family, or at least the male members of it, have rejected him as insane or possibly demon possessed. They stand aloof from him, and none of them are numbered among his followers.

Mary finds herself caught in the middle, torn between her faith in and love for her firstborn, and the fierce rejection he has engendered among her other sons. She knows the secret of his divine conception and the prophetic words that were spoken over him. She witnessed the miracles and the angelic confirmation that surrounded the events of his birth. Mary believes—no, she knows—that her son Jesus is the Son of God. At her prompting, he performed his first miracle at Cana (John 2:1–12). Yet here she finds herself caught in the middle of this storm of opposition—opposition within her own family. Owing to this opposition, she can only follow Jesus at a distance. She is not numbered among the women who supported and accompanied Jesus and his roving apostolic band as recorded in Luke's Gospel:

> After this, Jesus traveled about from one town and village to another, proclaiming the good news of the kingdom of God. The Twelve were with him, and also

---

[33] Mark 3:20-34; see also Matthew 12:46-50 and Luke 8:19–21.

[34] John 1:11–13 and John 3:1–21.

[35] Matthew 10:34–39; see also Luke 14:26–27.

[36] Matthew 3:17, Mark 1:11, Luke 3:22.

some women who had been cured of evil spirits and diseases: Mary (called Magdalene) from whom seven demons had come out; Joanna the wife of Chuza, the manager of Herod's household; Susanna; and many others. These women were helping to support them out of their own means. (Luke 8:1–3)

Undoubtedly, Mary followed the reports of Jesus' ministry with great interest. Repeatedly the gospel accounts record how the news of Jesus' miraculous signs and healings spread throughout the entire region of Galilee and Judea. These reports would spur Mary to even greater faith. Surely the biblical prophecies were coming true. Her son was the long-awaited Messiah. His miraculous powers testified to his divinity. For Mary and thousands of others, hope tingled in the air. Israel's day of deliverance was drawing nigh.

It is amid this air of expectant hope that Mary set out from Galilee to celebrate the Passover in Jerusalem. This annual pilgrimage was a well-established family tradition.[37] Undoubtedly, she travelled in the company of one or more of her adult sons: James, Joseph, Simon, or Judas (Jude). No middle-aged woman at that time would undertake such a pilgrimage on her own.

Above all, Passover was and is a family celebration of the deliverance of the firstborn from the angel of death. It is a time for families to gather together. For Mary this journey would have brought back memories of that journey years earlier with her twelve-year-old firstborn, Jesus. Due to the rupture in relations recorded earlier, he was not part of the family gathering now. Jesus was with his new family, his disciples. He was going about *"his Father's business"*

(Luke 2:49). But his presence amidst the festive throng stirred their collective faith as never before. They sensed the anticipation. Surely, the long-awaited kingdom of God was at hand.

On the final morning of their journey, as they left Jericho for the ascent to Jerusalem, their hopes were confirmed. To the astonishment of

---

[37] *Every year Jesus' parents went to Jerusalem for the Festival of the Passover. When he was twelve years old, they went up to the festival, according to the custom.* (Luke 2:41–42)

all, Jesus performed one of his greatest miracles. Mark's gospel gives us the most lucid account:

> As Jesus and his disciples, together with a large crowd, were leaving the city, a blind man, Bartimaeus (which means "son of Timaeus"), was sitting by the roadside begging.
>
> When he heard that it was Jesus of Nazareth, he began to shout, "Jesus, Son of David, have mercy on me!"
>
> Many rebuked him and told him to be quiet, but he shouted all the more, "Son of David, have mercy on me!"
>
> Jesus stopped and said, "Call him."
>
> So they called to the blind man, "Cheer up! On your feet! He's calling you." Throwing his cloak aside, he jumped to his feet and came to Jesus.
>
> "What do you want me to do for you?" Jesus asked him.
>
> The blind man said, "Rabbi, I want to see."
>
> "Go," said Jesus, "your faith has healed you." Immediately he received his sight and followed Jesus along the road. (Mark 10:46–52)

The effect that this demonstration of heaven-sent power had upon the crowd cannot be overestimated. This was divine confirmation. The Messiah had come—was walking among them now! Deliverance was at hand. Surely, Jesus was the promised son of David—the anointed one—the Christ.

That morning Jesus did more than open the eyes of a beggar; he opened the eyes of the pilgrims to his divine call and mission. And as they continued their journey, that beggar, Bartimaeus, was walking, talking, living proof of the Messiah's power. A blind beggar, healed and set free, embodied the Passover pilgrims' hopes and dreams. They too could be set free from the bondage of Roman rule. Anything was possible. The kingdom of God was among them. The rightful king of the kingdom was walking the dusty road with them.

As they reached the outskirts of Jerusalem, the excitement built to a crescendo. Jesus climbed on the back of a commandeered donkey, and the crowd began to hail him as king. In doing this, he and his followers signaled that he was the coming Messiah-King, the Christ, spoken of in Old Testament prophecy.[38]

> Many people spread their cloaks on the road, while others spread branches they had cut in the fields. Those who went ahead and those who followed shouted,
> "Hosanna!"
> "Blessed is he who comes in the name of the Lord!"
> "Blessed is the coming kingdom of our father David!"
> "Hosanna in the highest heaven!" (Mark 11:8–10)

Mary's heart must have swelled with pride as this image unfolded. Her firstborn was being hailed as king! Before her very eyes the words of the angel Gabriel—the words of the annunciation—were coming true.

> He will be great and will be called the Son of the Most High. The Lord God will give him the throne of his father David, and he will reign over Jacob's descendants forever; his kingdom will never end. (Luke 1:32–33)

Only Caiaphas, the high priest, and Pontius Pilate, the Roman governor, stood in the way. All too soon these aspirations of greatness came crashing down. The soft power of a spiritual kingdom collided with the

---

[38] Rejoice greatly, Daughter Zion!
Shout, Daughter Jerusalem!
See, your king comes to you,
righteous and victorious,
lowly and riding on a donkey,
on a colt, the foal of a donkey. (Zechariah 9:9)

brute force of Rome. Though this grand arrival set all of Jerusalem in a stir,[39] the powers that be were not about to surrender authority and control to a so-called prophet from Nazareth.

Upon his arrival Jesus launched a coup. But the coup was not against the Romans. Instead, it was against the temple authorities. Jesus set about cleansing the temple compound of marketers and moneychangers, and then he turned it into his center for healing and teaching.[40] The high priestly clan would countenance none of this. The crafty Caiaphas plotted revenge.[41]

The week that began with a king on a donkey ended with a king on a cross.

For Mary the more ominous words of another prophet were about to come true. At the infant Jesus' dedication in the temple, the prophet Simeon had said to Mary, *"And a sword will pierce your own soul too"* (Luke 2:35b). The cruelest cut was yet to come.

Sunday's elation transitioned to midweek apprehension and finally Friday's death and despair. An incomprehensible reversal—an unfathomable descent into hell—that's what Mary experienced.

Her midmorning arrival at the foot of her son's cross evokes a level of pathos that breaks the bounds of description.

> Near the cross of Jesus stood his mother, his mother's sister, Mary the wife of Clopas, and Mary Magdalene. When Jesus saw his mother there, and the disciple whom he loved standing nearby, he said to her, "Woman, here is your son," and to the disciple, "Here is your mother." From that time on, this disciple took her into his home. (John 19:25–27)

Jesus committed his mother into the care of John, his dearest disciple, *"the disciple whom he loved."* This was the spoken will of a dying

---

[39] See Matthew 21:10–11.

[40] See Matthew 21:12–17.

[41] See John 11:47–53.

man, and according to the text above, Mary and John carried out Jesus' will. Mary moved into John's home.

This event raises a whole series of questions:

- Why would Jesus commit his mother into the care of his disciple?
- Why would Mary agree to this new living arrangement?
- Where were Jesus' brothers? Why are they not with their mother at the foot of the cross?

What was the motive and basis for this new living arrangement?

None of this makes sense unless there was a deep rift—an estrangement—between Jesus and his brothers. As we have already seen, such an estrangement was evident early on in Jesus' ministry. His crucifixion brought this rift fully into the open. Here was the climax—the final cut. The family is torn asunder. As for Mary, she has irrevocably aligned herself with Jesus, her firstborn.

But where is James in all this? Where are the other half-brothers? It is unimaginable or highly unlikely that James was not present in Jerusalem for this Passover. The Passover was a family celebration, and with Joseph's death, and Jesus' abandonment or abdication of his family responsibilities, James was now the head of the home.[42] Since we know Mary did not come to Jerusalem with Jesus and his apostolic band, we must conclude that she came with James. As the oldest son of Joseph, it was his responsibility to lead the family in the sacred celebration of deliverance from the bondage of Egypt through the blood of the Passover lamb.

It is reasonable to believe that while Jesus was celebrating his last Passover meal and instituting the communion sacrament with his spiritual family—his disciples in Jerusalem—James was leading the Passover celebration with Mary his mother and Jesus' natural family members at another location in the city. The house of Joseph was divided.

---

[42] It is unclear from the scriptural account, whether Jesus abandoned his role as head of the family in order to pursue his call to ministry, or perhaps James usurped his older brother's authority and pushed him out of the family nest.

James was not present at the communion table because clearly there was no spiritual union between him and Jesus. By instituting this sacrament Jesus established a link between his imminent death—as the paschal lamb offered up for the sins of the world—and the ancient Jewish Passover ritual. But there is a deeper meaning in this blood sacrifice that warrants further exploration.

Using the emblems of bread and wine, Jesus commanded his disciples to eat his body and drink his blood. Though his words should be interpreted figuratively or spiritually,[43] they nonetheless represent a drastic departure from orthodox Jewish teaching. Human sacrifice is universally condemned under the Old Covenant, and though the meat of the sacrificial animal or paschal lamb was consumed, by a direct command of God the blood must never be. *"And wherever you live, you must not eat the blood of any bird or animal. Anyone who eats blood must be cut off from their people"* (Leviticus 7:26–27).

The prohibition is sharp.

According to John's Gospel, Jesus introduced this teaching about eating his body and drinking his blood in the town of Capernaum in Galilee, prior to instituting the sacrament at his last Passover in Jerusalem. Not surprisingly, his teaching was roundly rejected at that time.

> Jesus said to them, "Very truly I tell you, unless you eat the flesh of the Son of Man and drink his blood, you have no life in you. Whoever eats my flesh and drinks my blood has eternal life, and I will raise them up at the last day. For my flesh is real food and my blood is real drink. Whoever eats my flesh and drinks my blood remains in me, and I in them. Just as the living Father sent me and I live because of the Father, so the one who feeds on me will live because of me. This is the bread that came down from heaven. Your ancestors ate manna and died, but whoever feeds on this bread will live

---

[43] In explaining the language or terms he is using in describing the eating of his flesh and drinking of his blood, Jesus states the following: *"The Spirit gives life; the flesh counts for nothing. The words I have spoken to you—they are full of the Spirit and life"* (John 6:63).

forever." He said this while teaching in the synagogue in Capernaum. (John 6:53–59)

The thought of eating human flesh and drinking human blood is disgusting, repulsive, and strictly forbidden in religious law. The response of the faithful in Capernaum should surprise no one. "*On hearing it, many of his disciples said, 'This is a hard teaching. Who can accept it?'*" (John 6:60)

John goes on to report the effect that this teaching had on his followers. "*From this time many of his disciples turned back and no longer followed him*" (John 6:66).

The question that naturally springs to mind is: Why introduce such a disturbing teaching? Why attempt to overthrow centuries of religious law?

Clearly Jesus must have attached a great deal of significance to this doctrine. It was not peripheral; it was at the core of his teaching. Furthermore, it was at the core of his teaching because it was at the core of his being. It was about his DNA—divine eternal DNA being transferred to his followers. This is why Jesus says, "*Whoever eats my flesh and drinks my blood remains in me, and I in them. Just as the living Father sent me and I live because of the Father, so the one who feeds on me will live because of me*" (John 6:56–57).

Eternity was written into Christ's DNA, and to have eternal life, his followers must have eternal DNA. Eternal DNA is found in the blood of Christ. That is why in the sacrament he offers his blood to his followers. In his blood is the life of God. In communion, on a symbolic spiritual level, we become partakers in the DNA of Christ.

To impart eternal life to his disciples, which is only available through his shed blood, Jesus overturns the centuries' old Levitical prohibition against consuming blood:

> For the life of a creature is in the blood, and I have given it to you to make atonement for yourselves on the altar; it is the blood that makes atonement for one's life. (Leviticus 17:11)

Not only did Jesus' followers need to partake in his divine DNA, but they also needed to be cleansed by and forgiven through the sacrifice of his body. His shed blood atones for their sins, making them acceptable to God their Father. The writer of the Book of Hebrews makes this concept clear when he states, "*In fact, the law requires that nearly everything be cleansed with blood, and without the shedding of blood there is no forgiveness*" (Hebrews 9:21–23).

Forgiveness and eternal life are available now through the body and blood of Christ for all who believe. But at this point in our narrative James does not believe. He stands outside the family of God as described by his half-brother, the Lamb of God. James has not experienced a spiritual rebirth. To him this talk of consuming his brother's flesh and blood is the gibberish of a madman—or worse yet, highhanded blasphemy.

While Jesus instituted the holy sacrament, James, the firstborn son of Joseph, celebrated the Jewish Passover in the traditional way. As a dutiful mother and the family matriarch, Mary would be present with James. But her heart was with Jesus—her firstborn. After all, this memorial celebration was all about the firstborn who was protected from the Angel of Death by the blood of the Passover lamb.

The spiritual family and the natural family of Jesus celebrated the Passover in strikingly different ways. For the most part, this is a difference that continues to this day, as Passover and the celebration of the Eucharist mark the dividing line between the Jewish and Christian faith.

The very next morning, though James was present in the city, he refused to come with his mother to the foot of the cross. As his half-brother Jesus, the Lamb of God, hung dying, James would not climb the hill of Golgotha to bid him farewell. That is how intense the animosity he felt toward Jesus was. James shunned and despised Jesus in the moment of his greatest suffering—in the moment of his death.

Undoubtedly, before Mary arrived at the foot of the cross, there was an intense and heated conversation between her and James. This conversation is not recorded in scripture; it happened off-camera, so to speak. But it's not difficult to imagine the issues at play.

Mary is caught in the jaws of this horrific turn of events. Mary's soaring hopes and dreams for her messianic son have come crashing to the ground. Her faith is shattered. Heaven's promise has turned into hell—an intensely personal hell. In her grief, her only thought is to spend a few final minutes with the child she bore, the child she nursed and loved—the son of her most cherished dreams.

James on the other hand is seized with a mixture of anguish and rage. He sees his brother's crucifixion as a natural consequence flowing from the words and actions of a dangerously deluded mind. He had tried to put an end to this messianic delusion—to take charge of his brother early in his ministry—all to no avail (Mark 3:20–35). Now his worst nightmare has come to pass. And what had all this talk of the kingdom of God accomplished? It led directly to death on a Roman cross—an outcome that was entirely predictable. Wasn't this the reason he tried to take charge of Jesus? But the deluded fool would have none of it. He refused to listen to his family and the voice of reason.

As seen through the eyes of James, the sins of Jesus were numerous and stunningly heinous. He abandoned his family responsibilities. He rejected the wise counsel of his family members; in fact, he rejected his entire family.[44] From the earliest days of his ministry, Jesus was a deranged rebel, who opposed the highest religious authorities in the land.[45] Furthermore, he had the audacity to take his opposition to authority to the highest level. He denounced the strict and pious Pharisees, men whose legal scruples James admired. But not content with mocking the religious establishment from the sidelines, Jesus invaded the temple courts with his deluded hordes and challenged the authority of the high priest in his own precinct. Is it any wonder that Caiaphas reacted as he did?

But here is the most grievous of all his transgressions. Jesus had delusions of grandeur—of Deity. How could James' brother—his flesh and blood brother—be God? Deity come in the flesh? Preposterous! Such an

---

[44] *"Who are my mother and my brothers?" he [Jesus] asked. Then he looked at those seated in a circle around him and said, "Here are my mother and my brothers! Whoever does God's will is my brother and sister and mother."* (Mark 3:33–35).

[45] *And the teachers of the law who came down from Jerusalem said, "He [Jesus] is possessed by Beelzebul! By the prince of demons he is driving out demons."* (Mark 3:22).

idea was beyond scandalous. It was the height of blasphemy. And James was proven right in this assessment when the Jewish high council, the Sanhedrin, reached its verdict in Jesus' trial.[46]

What might James have thought at this moment? *Death on a cross was too kind an outcome for such a fool—such a bastard!*

And now Mary, the mother of this bastard—yes, and his own mother too—wants to say farewell to her bastard. Well, let her go. She was the mother of this bastard, and for reasons that totally confounded James, she had urged Jesus on in this course of action—this blasphemous folly to the shame and disgrace of the entire family.

Let her go. Let her go crying to her humiliated, bastard son. Wasn't she the mother of this catastrophe—this affront to the Jewish faith? She was the source and the root cause of all the dissension in the family. From the moment of Jesus' conception to this very instant, Mary had brought disrepute and an immeasurable dishonour to the house of Joseph.

Let the b*tch go to her bastard now, he must have thought.[47] But in all likelihood, James also let Mary know that if she went to see Jesus, she was unwelcome in his home. If she went crying to him—if she sided with him—she too was an outcast.

This is a look into the mind of James on the day Jesus died.

Well, Mary made her decision. She walked to the foot of the cross. But she did not come forward alone. She came with other believers, her sister, *"Mary the wife of Clopas, and Mary Magdalene."*[48] At last Mary has fully entered the circle of Jesus followers. She made a courageous and conscientious decision to associate herself with the family of God. She aligned herself with her firstborn.

---

[46] *Again the high priest asked him [Jesus], "Are you the Messiah, the Son of the Blessed One?" "I am," said Jesus. "And you will see the Son of Man sitting at the right hand of the Mighty One and coming on the clouds of heaven."*

The high priest tore his clothes. "Why do we need any more witnesses?" he asked. "You have heard the blasphemy. What do you think?" They all condemned him as worthy of death. (Mark 14:61b–64)

[47] I derive no pleasure in using these derogatory terms. Strong, insulting language is used here to signal the complete breakdown of the family relationship.

[48] See John 19:25.

Why did Jesus commit his mother into John's care? Without this background, this decision makes no sense because Mary has four remaining sons—and daughters, as well. According to rabbinical law and practice, the oldest son was required to be her provider in her declining years as a widow. The decision to commit Mary to John's care only makes sense in view of the scenario that has just been described. Mary needs a new home and a new family because she has been rejected by her remaining children, her own flesh and blood.

Mary stood before Jesus as a homeless widow without a family. She is not an orphan in the traditional sense of the word, but with the death of Jesus, she will become an orphan from her natural family. Therefore, Jesus entrusts her into John's care.

With her arrival at the cross, Mary has taken on a new identity in the fullest sense imaginable, even as Jesus did when he was baptized. She has left the household of Joseph and joined the household of God. She will be forever known as the mother of the Son of God.

Jesus would not leave his mother in the care of an unbeliever, so he entrusted her to John, his dearest disciple.

There is a profound spiritual dynamic at work here. Jesus is signaling to all that spiritual birth takes precedence over natural birth. In his eternal kingdom, the spiritual family and spiritual DNA trump the natural family and natural DNA.

For Mary this was the final cut. She was cut off from her natural family and grafted into the family tree of God.

---— 8 ——

The Resurrection Restoration

The cataclysmic events of Good Friday left a shattered, fragmented family in its wake. On one level James must have felt vindicated. He had rightly assessed the pitfalls and dangers in his elder brother's radical messianic mission. At times, he may have felt a kind of 'I-told-you-so' triumphalism. But there was no joy in it. How could there be? His brother was dead, the family lay in ruins, and the family reputation among the elite of Jewish society was in tatters—totally beyond redemption.

Family reputation meant a great deal to James. Saving face and maintaining family honour has always been of primary significance in Middle Eastern culture. How could James show his face back in Nazareth, knowing that his brother had been crucified for blasphemy and treason?

After all, the Sanhedrin had found Jesus guilty of blasphemy.[49] From the outset of his ministry Jesus had dared to preach about the emergent kingdom of God.[50] For the folly of this message he would die. Jesus and his message challenged the authority of Rome. A crown of thorns

---

[49] See Mark 14:61b–64.

[50] *After John was put in prison, Jesus went into Galilee, proclaiming the good news of God. "The time has come," he said. "The kingdom of God has come near. Repent and believe the good news!"* (Mark 1:14–15)

was Rome's answer for such audacity. John's gospel account gives us the clearest picture of how this charge of treason played itself out:

> From then on, Pilate tried to set Jesus free, but the Jewish leaders kept shouting, "If you let this man go, you are no friend of Caesar. Anyone who claims to be a king opposes Caesar."
>
> When Pilate heard this, he brought Jesus out and sat down on the judge's seat at a place known as the Stone Pavement (which in Aramaic is Gabbatha). It was the day of Preparation of the Passover; it was about noon.
>
> "Here is your king," Pilate said to the Jews.
>
> But they shouted, "Take him away! Take him away! Crucify him!"
>
> "Shall I crucify your king?" Pilate asked.
>
> "We have no king but Caesar," the chief priests answered.
>
> Finally Pilate handed him over to them to be crucified. (John 19:12–16)

During the trial Pontius Pilate played his cards shrewdly. In exchange for a guilty verdict, he extracted what he had long wanted from the chief priests: a pledge of fidelity to Rome.

The humiliation and disgrace of the cross stained a family's reputation immeasurably. Present day readers may easily underestimate the significance of this humiliation. Crosses adorn churches and are hung on gold chains around our necks. The cross is commonly used as jewelry. For us it has lost its horror. It is a symbol of faith and hope. Not so for the first century citizen of the Roman Empire. For the people of that day, it was viewed with revulsion. They saw it for what it was: a heinous instrument of death.

As the family head, James bore the shame of the cross. His errant bastard brother had brought shame to the family name. Jesus was stripped naked and pinned to a cross along the Roman road into the city. His crime was posted above his head: The King of the Jews. There he hung for all to see—a public spectacle—a living, dying billboard displaying his arrogance and the error of his ways.

It was more than James could bear. Some might understand or sympathize with someone charged with treason against Rome, but blasphemy against God was another matter. It was beyond the pale—an affront to the faith—an affront to the family's Jewish identity. James could not countenance the thought.

To protect himself and his younger brothers, James took the drastic measure of disowning his mother. The elders in the community of Nazareth already recognized that Mary had conceived Jesus in sin. With Jesus' trial and crucifixion, the rumours of old gained fresh currency. This child was conceived out of wedlock. He was not the son of Joseph. No son of Joseph would drag the family name through such a slough of infamy. Bad seed brings forth a bad harvest. And this outcome—this public crucifixion—was the ultimate in a bad harvest.

During Jesus' ministry years, James had done what he could to distance himself from his older brother. Now that Jesus' renown had turned into shame, he cut the final cord. He repudiated his mother. Surely the synagogue elders in Nazareth would approve of his actions. What else could he do to expunge this stain from the family record?

Three years earlier, after a hostile reception in his hometown, Jesus spoke these words, "*A prophet is not without honor except in his own country, among his own relatives, and in his own house*" (Mark 6:4, NKJV). Jesus the prophet spoke the truth. His own household rejected him.

As he hung dying, he cried out, "*'Eloi, Eloi, lama sabachthani?' which is translated, 'My God, My God, why have You forsaken Me?'*" (Mark 15:34b, NKJV)

In his moment of greatest anguish, Jesus was rejected by his earthly family, his disciples had scattered in fear, and apparently even his heavenly Father had abandoned him. The physical torment of the cross was coupled with the torment of utter rejection on every level.

James turned his back on his brother—so much for brotherly love. Surely, this was the low point. Between them, things could sink no lower. Does hell have a basement?

And yet… And yet the story does not end there. If we read through the remainder of the New Testament, we discover that James—this same James, the brother of Jesus—becomes a prominent leader in the early church. In fact, he authored a much quoted, canonical book that bears his name. How could this be?

The short answer is because of the resurrection. The resurrection changed everything, including the trajectory of James' life.

There are certain stories in the New Testament that get a lot of play. By that I mean they are well known. The writer or writers provide the reader with a lot of information. The narrative is rich in detail, and in several instances, particularly in the gospels, we hear the account from various perspectives. The story of Paul's conversion is told twice in the Book of Acts, for example, and snippets of it can be found in Paul's epistles.

The conversion of James is not like that. We would know nothing of it except for a cursory mention that appears in Paul's first letter to the Corinthians. Most casual readers pay little attention to this passing reference. But in accounting for the change in the life of James, this passage has enormous significance.

In Paul's great defence of the resurrection, he makes this statement:

> For what I received I passed on to you as of first importance: that Christ died for our sins according to the Scriptures, that he was buried, that he was raised on the third day according to the Scriptures, and that he appeared to Cephas [Peter], and then to the Twelve. After that, he appeared to more than five hundred of the brothers and sisters at the same time, most of whom are still living, though some have fallen asleep. Then he appeared to James, then to all the apostles, and last of all he appeared to me also, as to one abnormally born. (1 Corinthians 15:3–7)

The resurrected Christ appeared to James! What an astonishing experience that must have been! It most certainly changed his life—altered his belief system—rattled his cage to the core. James had an encounter with his resurrected brother. For an unbeliever—more than that, an enemy of the gospel message—this can only be a trauma of the highest magnitude.

Imagine the scene for a moment. James is back in Nazareth in his carpentry shop working on some project. Perhaps his head is down, focussed on his work. He looks up and to his astonishment Jesus is there. The brother he believes is dead is standing before him.

Presumably, words are exchanged. What did Jesus say? How did James respond? This side of eternity we will never know the answer, but surely this was the most pivotal event in the life of James. Without question, it was also a pivotal event in the life of the early church.

Did Jesus show James the nail scars in his hands and feet? Did James require visible and tactile proof, as was the case with the apostle Thomas?[51] No one knows for sure; the biblical record is silent. What we do know with certainty is that from that moment on James was totally transformed. He was now firmly in the camp of the believers.

In a single encounter, the enmity that tore the family apart was reversed. It takes a miracle to restore a severed relationship. It took a miracle in the order of magnitude of the resurrection to re-establish this poisoned brotherly relationship.

The significance of this turning point should not be underestimated. There is ample evidence to support the concept that the conversion of James shaped not only the history of the early church, but the entire world.

---

[51] See John 20:24–29.

9

Resurrection Visitation—When and Why

The cataclysmic events of Good Friday left a shattered, fragmented family in its wake. In the wake of Easter Sunday, Jesus' post-resurrection visit with James was undoubtedly aimed at restoring a healthy family relationship. There is every indication that this visitation accomplished its purpose.

Because this event is so pivotal in the life of James moving forward, it warrants a closer examination. The New Testament information is indeed scant, but it is possible to propose a sequenced time frame for when this critical meeting of the two brothers took place.

First, we need to use Paul the apostle's statement in 1 Corinthians as a guide. It is repeated here for quick reference:

> For what I received I passed on to you as of first importance: that Christ died for our sins according to the Scriptures, that he was buried, that he was raised on the third day according to the Scriptures, and that he appeared to Cephas [Peter], and then to the Twelve. After that, he appeared to more than five hundred of the brothers and sisters at the same time, most of whom are still living, though some have fallen asleep. Then he appeared to James, then to all the apostles, and

last of all he appeared to me also, as to one abnormally
born. (1 Corinthians 15:3–7)

It should however be noted that Paul's account of the resurrection
appearances of Christ is not comprehensive or complete. It was not intended to be an exhaustive listing of these events. The gospel writers
detail other appearances that are not recorded in Paul's defence of the
resurrection. For example, Paul makes no mention of the three women
who first reported the resurrection to the apostles on Sunday morning,[52]
nor does he report the more personal encounter between Jesus and Mary
Magdalene.[53] The gospel writers Luke and Mark report on Jesus' encounter with two disciples on the road to Emmaus on Sunday afternoon
and evening.[54] This was followed later that evening by his appearing to
the eleven in a room with other gathered followers,[55] though apparently
Thomas was not present. Eight days later Jesus appeared again among
the apostles, and he made a point of convincing Thomas that the story
of his resurrection was not a fabrication.

John's account of this incident bears repeating here, since it may have
been similar in some respects to Christ's encounter with his half-brother
James.

> Now Thomas (also known as Didymus), one of the
> Twelve, was not with the disciples when Jesus came. So
> the other disciples told him, "We have seen the Lord!"
> But he said to them, "Unless I see the nail marks in
> his hands and put my finger where the nails were, and
> put my hand into his side, I will not believe."
> A week later his disciples were in the house again,
> and Thomas was with them. Though the doors were
> locked, Jesus came and stood among them and said,

---

[52] Luke 24:1–11, Mark 16:1–8, Matthew 28:1–10.

[53] Mark 16:9, John 20:10–18.

[54] Mark 16:12–13, Luke 24:13–35.

[55] Mark 16:14, Luke 24:33–43, John 20:19–23.

"Peace be with you!" Then he said to Thomas, "Put your finger here; see my hands. Reach out your hand and put it into my side. Stop doubting and believe."

Thomas said to him, "My Lord and my God!"

Then Jesus told him, "Because you have seen me, you have believed; blessed are those who have not seen and yet have believed." (John 20:24–29)

Did James need this type of hands-on encounter to convince him that Jesus was alive, was standing before him and had risen from the dead? It certainly seems likely, since the apostle John called him an unbeliever (John 7:5). Did the brothers share a meal together, thus proving that the risen Jesus had fleshly substance and was not merely a ghostly apparition?[56]

Sometimes the most difficult people to persuade are the members of our own family. They know us too well and are fully aware of our foibles and shortcomings. After all, familiarity breeds contempt. But another familial phenomenon may be at play here. When we acknowledge the strengths of our sibling, we may feel diminished before them. Having seized the leadership role in the household of Joseph, did James begrudge yielding any authority or praise to the brother whose position he usurped? From James' perspective, he was not usurping Jesus' position. He was simply assuming his lawful role as the firstborn heir of Joseph. But acknowledging one's brother as Messiah and Deity is a steep step down for any man to take. Bending the knee would not come easily.

James was a difficult nut to crack. There was a hard exterior to him built up over years of rivalry, personal pride, and ambition. Those who have read his New Testament epistle will readily acknowledge that James

---

[56] *While they were still talking about this, Jesus himself stood among them and said to them, "Peace be with you."*

They were startled and frightened, thinking they saw a ghost. He said to them, "Why are you troubled, and why do doubts rise in your minds? Look at my hands and my feet. It is I myself! Touch me and see; a ghost does not have flesh and bones, as you see I have."

When he had said this, he showed them his hands and feet. And while they still did not believe it because of joy and amazement, he asked them, "Do you have anything here to eat?" They gave him a piece of broiled fish, and he took it and ate it in their presence. (Luke 24:36–42)

was a man of rock-solid conviction and impeccable zeal. Some of those characteristics were undoubted evident before his conversion. They were simply oriented in a different direction—a direction that was hostile to Jesus and his mission. In this respect, James was very similar to another New Testament character—Saul who after his encounter with the risen Christ became the zealous apostle Paul.

James the skeptic would certainly need proof of the resurrection. If stunning proof was what he needed, Jesus was willing to provide it.

Luke, the author of the Book of Acts, informs us that there was a forty-day window—from the resurrection to Christ's ascension—within which the encounter with James must have occurred.

> In my former book, Theophilus, I wrote about all that Jesus began to do and to teach until the day he was taken up to heaven, after giving instructions through the Holy Spirit to the apostles he had chosen. After his suffering, he presented himself to them and gave many convincing proofs that he was alive. He appeared to them over a period of forty days and spoke about the kingdom of God. (Acts 2:1–3)

When this passage is compared with Paul's remarks on the resurrection in 1 Corinthians 15, it becomes clear that Christ's visitation with James took place near the conclusion of this forty-day period. Jesus saved the encounter with his fiercest skeptic and rival until near the end. Why would this be the case?

One can reasonably assume that there was some logical plan to the appearances that Jesus made. He was providing visible, physical proof of his resurrection. Luke says just that in the Acts passage cited above.

There is also a trainload of significance to the fact that these appearances happened over a period of forty days. Throughout the scriptures the passage of forty days signals a time of testing or proving. The great flood in the days of Noah took place over forty days (Genesis 7:17). Moses spent forty days with God on Mount Sinai receiving the Law (Exodus 34:28). Elijah traveled forty days to Mount Horeb, the mountain of God, on the strength of a single meal (1 Kings 19:7-9). In the same way, Jesus fasted forty days in the wilderness where he was tempted by the devil.[57] He was severely tested before his public ministry began. During that time of testing, Jesus proved that he was victorious over a triumvirate of evil—the temptations of the flesh, the world and the devil. He proved that he was ready to take on the responsibility of his redemptive mission.

Jesus' life on planet earth was bookended by another forty days of proving. During this final forty-day interval, he went about proving that he had overcome another triumvirate that rules all humanity—the triumvirate of death, hell and the grave.

Despite repeatedly prophesying this very outcome,[58] Jesus' physical resurrection was greeted with profound astonishment and near-universal skepticism. An excerpt from Mark's gospel account dramatically illustrates this point:

> When Jesus rose early on the first day of the week, he appeared first to Mary Magdalene, out of whom he had driven seven demons. She went and told those who had been with him and who were mourning and weeping. When they heard that Jesus was alive and that she had seen him, they did not believe it.
>
> Afterward Jesus appeared in a different form to two of them while they were walking in the country. These returned and reported it to the rest; but they did not believe them either.
>
> Later Jesus appeared to the Eleven as they were eating; he rebuked them for their lack of faith and their stubborn refusal to believe those who had seen him after he had risen. (Mark 16:9–14)

One of the strongest arguments for the truth of the four gospel accounts springs from the unbelief of the apostles. When Jesus was raised from the dead, they were completely taken aback. Words such as floored,

---

[57] Matthew 4:1–11, Mark 1:12–13, Luke 4:1–13.

[58] See Mark 8:31–33, 9:30–32, 10:32–34.

dumbfounded and thunderstruck spring to mind. And well they should. This is a miracle that defies all the norms of human experience. Their initial unbelief paints a rather unflattering picture of the apostles. This down-to-earth realism, however, lends credibility to the gospel accounts. Who would not be incredulous at reports of someone who was horribly tortured and killed, publicly speared, and drained of his blood (John 19:33–35) suddenly rising from the dead?

Furthermore, anyone who has read the four gospel accounts of the resurrection will discover that there is a certain amount of disorderly chaos in the way the events are reported. They do not match perfectly, and on certain points they seem contradictory. Clearly, no one employed a fact checker before each of the gospels went to press. But rather than sully their credibility, this rather haphazard reporting lends credence to the truth of the events. The gospel accounts are not carefully crafted documents created by committee and verified in advance by scholarly research. On the contrary, they are independently produced, eyewitness accounts of events that transpired thirty-five or more years prior to the date when they were penned. Some discrepancies can be expected and indeed they are present. But rather than discredit the gospels, these straightforward recollections add to their authenticity and realism.

Present-day eyewitness accounts of the same event usually vary considerably in scope and detail. Witnesses whose stories agree perfectly provide evidence of collusion, nothing more. Discrepancies occur because each witness views the event from a different perspective and with varying degrees of perception. Also, human recall of an event is fallible and can vary over time. This is precisely what we encounter when we read the gospels. When one compares the resurrection accounts in the four gospels, some details appear to be jumbled or missing, but the picture that emerges is strong and clear: To the astonishment of all, Jesus rose from the dead.

Jesus had forty days to prove his resurrection. What logical plan did he follow to convince his followers, and ultimately the world, that he is alive?

Merely appearing before people who do not know him would prove nothing. They were not acquainted with him. Any random stranger could claim to have returned from the dead, but this claim means nothing to the hearer. It seems absurd! They do not know the man and they are unable to verify his claim. Nail scars in hands and feet may be curious features, but they could be self-inflicted wounds. They do not prove that the person thus wounded has risen from the dead.

The point of this argument is this: the people that Jesus must convince are his followers and those who knew him best. They are the only ones who can verify that this man, Jesus, rose from the dead. The general public, despite his fame, cannot verify that the resurrected Jesus is the same person who was put to death. Only those who knew him well can do that. For this reason, Jesus must convince his disciples—specifically the remaining eleven apostles. (Judas had hung himself.)[59] But what is even more important, he must convince his family—his unbelieving brothers. They knew him from his childhood to the point of his death. If he cannot convince them, Jesus has utterly failed in his mission. His resurrection will be deemed a lie—nothing more than a fabrication of his deluded followers. This is why police have a family member confirm the identify of an accident or murder victim.

Convincing James is then the ultimate test. Without James and the unbelieving brothers on side, the doctrine of the resurrection is a house of cards. To refute the resurrection claim, the brothers can simply testify that Jesus is dead. It is likely that they too saw him die from a distance. Since his crucifixion was a public event, along a public thoroughfare, it can be said with some accuracy that all Jerusalem witnessed his death.

Furthermore, the brothers can assert that his disciples are babbling idiots. They were already convinced of that before the crucifixion. Now the apostles have removed all doubt by spreading this wild fantasy about Jesus rising from the dead. To convince any thinking person from the public that Jesus is alive, his brothers must first be convinced that he is alive.

James is the linchpin. Unless he is converted, the entire gospel mission is stymied—dead on arrival. James is pivotal to the birth of the church and the advance of the gospel message. At the very core of the gospel message is the death, burial and resurrection of Jesus. For this reason, Jesus must prove to James that he has risen from the dead. He must prove that he is

---

[59] See Matthew 27:3–5.

the Son of God. If Jesus is unable to convince the members of his own family, how can the apostles expect to convince the world?

What use or purpose is there in a dead Savior? If he is not alive, the Christian faith is vain and lifeless as a corpse. It is as the apostle Paul says, "*And if Christ has not been raised, our preaching is useless and so is your faith*" (1 Corinthians 15:14). Only a living Savior can forgive sins and cleanse a guilt-stained heart. Only a living Savior can throw open heaven's gates. Only the resurrection fixes forever the Father's seal of approval on the Son. If Jesus remains dead, his death is deserved. If he rises from the dead, his life and his message are vindicated. He is who he said he was—the Son of the Most High.[60]

In addition, the gospel message is a message of reconciliation. Humanity is reconciled to God and to one another through the message of the gospel. Again, Paul sheds light on this central tenet of the gospel:

> Therefore, if anyone is in Christ, the new creation has come: The old has gone, the new is here! All this is from God, who reconciled us to himself through Christ and gave us the ministry of reconciliation: that God was reconciling the world to himself in Christ, not counting people's sins against them. And he has committed to us the message of reconciliation. (1 Corinthians 5:17–19)

The message of reconciliation rings hollow if Christ cannot be reconciled to his brothers. How can the practitioners of the gospel advocate for reconciliation if the founder of the faith could not be reconciled with the members of his own household? Reconciliation is applied forgiveness. Forgiveness is at the heart of Christ's teaching, and consequently reconciliation with James is essential. In a post-resurrection world, Jesus and James must be reconciled.

The gospel accounts bear witness to the urgency that Jesus attached to this mission of converting his brothers. On the night of his betrayal, he predicted that his disciples would desert him.

---

[60] Matthew 27:63–64, Luke 22:67–71.

"You will all fall away," Jesus told them, "for it is written:
"'I will strike the shepherd, and the sheep will be
scattered.'

"But after I have risen, I will go ahead of you into
Galilee." (Mark 14:27–28)

In announcing the resurrection, the angel at the tomb reiterates the
same instruction:

"Don't be alarmed," he said. "You are looking for Jesus
the Nazarene, who was crucified. He has risen! He is
not here. See the place where they laid him. But go, tell
his disciples and Peter, 'He is going ahead of you into
Galilee. There you will see him, just as he told you.'"
(Mark 16:6–7)

Jesus appeared later that day to Mary Magdalene, the tomb-visiting
women, to Peter, to two disciples on the road to Emmaus, and finally to
the apostles (minus Thomas) at their evening meal in Jerusalem. What
urgency was there then in returning to Galilee?

Galilee was the center point of Jesus' ministry. But, more than that,
it was his home. Once again, he would meet with his disciples there. But
more importantly, he would return home and meet with his brothers.
He says precisely that when he encounters the women near the tomb:

So the women hurried away from the tomb, afraid yet
filled with joy, and ran to tell his disciples. Suddenly Jesus met them. "Greetings," he said. They came to him,
clasped his feet and worshiped him. Then Jesus said to
them, "Do not be afraid. Go and tell my brothers to go
to Galilee; there they will see me." (Matthew 28:8–10)

The use of the term brothers (*adelphos* in Greek) is quite curious
here. By using this term, Jesus could be broadly referring to his disciples,
and most commentators interpret the word in this way. But why would

Jesus say this if he was seeing his disciples that evening? Could he also be using the term brothers in the traditional familial sense of the word? Was he instructing these women to tell his unbelieving brothers and related kin to return to Galilee, where he will meet with them again?

His instruction for the brothers to return to Galilee also signals an end to the mourning period. Traditionally, Jewish families are expected to sit for seven days while mourning the loss of their deceased family member. But Jesus was no longer dead, so his announcement to the two Marys (Matthew 28:1-8) was a declaration of an end to the mourning period. Since he was alive, the family members *(adelphos)* who were in Jerusalem were free to return home to Galilee. The Jewish *shiv-ah* (mourning period) was over, because the deceased was very much alive.

Typically, the first day of the week, Sunday, was a travel day for the Passover pilgrims. With the end of the Passover week and the final Sabbath, the pilgrims would begin the long journey home. Jesus' family members in Jerusalem had delayed their departure because of his death. They were observing *shiv-ah*. Now these two women give the brothers, his mother and other relatives the message that Jesus is alive. He will meet them in Galilee. What a startling turn of events this must have been for James!

The report of Jesus' words must have cut to the core. *"Do not be afraid. Go and tell my brothers to go to Galilee; there they will see me"* (Matthew 28:10).

It would seem clear that these words were not intended solely for the eleven apostles. They would see Jesus that evening. They were also intended for his natural *adelphos*—his brothers according to the flesh.

Did James go to the empty tomb, even as Peter and John did?[61] Did he believe the disciples stole Jesus' body away?[62] What did he make of the reports of his brother's resurrection? Surely word of it spread like wildfire.

That evening Jesus appeared to his huddled and perplexed disciples. But he did not appear to James, since according to Paul's defence

---

[61] John 20:2–10.

[62] Matthew 28:11–15.

of the resurrection in 1 Corinthians 15 that meeting was reserved for a later date.

Why was the meeting with James delayed? Paul's list of resurrection appearances provides us with some clues. It would seem Jesus reserved the hard cases to the end.

Broadly speaking, it would seem that Jesus' resurrection appearances moved outward in concentric rings from his inner circle, to the outer circle of disciples, to the doubters, and finally the openly hostile. Peter and Mary Magdalene were certainly in the closest inner ring. The Eleven comprise the next circle and then come other disciples beyond the apostolic band. Thomas represents the classic doubter, but there certainly were others, unmentioned by name in the scriptures, who presumably fit in this category. Paul and James fall in the category of the openly hostile—Paul for his persecution of the church, James because of his apparent opposition to Jesus and his gospel message.

As the evidence mounted and testimonials that Jesus was alive kept coming in, it must have produced a great deal of consternation in the hostile, unbelieving James. Since the great rift had opened between them, he had lived his life as a counterpoint to Jesus. These polar opposites did not attract.

In due course, Jesus met with his disciples in Galilee. This included his early morning seaside breakfast meeting with several of them. This occurred after Peter had led the group in a return-to-their-roots fishing expedition. Jesus took this occasion to fully restore his relationship with Peter after his threefold denial on the night of his betrayal. Three times Jesus asked Peter if he loved him, and three times Peter responded in the affirmative (John 21:1-19).

It seems only fitting that Jesus would do the same work of restoration and reconciliation with James. Did it take only one meeting, or were there several? We do not know. They met at least once according to Paul's testimony. It took several meetings before the relationship with Peter was fully restored. It seems reasonable to postulate that Jesus spent a good deal of time with James and his brothers. Their relationship was in much greater need of repair. They had a great deal to talk about. Of those forty post-resurrection days, a good many may have been spent with family, renewing ties that had been damaged and frayed almost beyond repair.

It only seems logical that Jesus returned to Galilee and to his family to rebuild a bridge across a great divide. As we will see, there is ample evidence that he succeeded.

—— Part Two ——
James the Leader
James through the Lens of the Book of Acts

—— 10 ——

Out of the Shadows a Leader Emerges

The most reliable account that we have of the early days of the church is Luke's New Testament book known as *The Acts of the Apostles* (commonly abbreviated to Acts). It is the primary source through which we discover James' spectacular rise to prominence in the church at Jerusalem.

Acts gives us a well-researched depiction of the explosive growth of the infant church. In his last meeting with the apostles just before his bodily ascension into heaven, Jesus predicts how the gospel message will ripple out from Jerusalem in concentric circles like waves in a pond after a rock has dropped into it.

> Then they [the apostles] gathered around him and asked him, "Lord, are you at this time going to restore the kingdom to Israel?"
>
> He [Jesus] said to them: "It is not for you to know the times or dates the Father has set by his own authority. But you will receive power when the Holy Spirit comes on you; and you will be my witnesses in Jerusalem, and in all Judea and Samaria, and to the ends of the earth." (Acts 1:6–8)

Essentially, the above statement is a quick outline of the Book of Acts. Through the chronological progression of twenty-eight chapters, Luke describes the advance of the gospel message from Jerusalem, through Judea, to Samaria, and finally, through the ministry of the apostle Paul, to the ends of the earth. The book ends with Paul the apostle boldly preaching the message of Christ—his life, death, burial, and resurrection—while awaiting his own trial before Caesar in Rome.

> For two whole years Paul stayed there in his own rented house and welcomed all who came to see him. He proclaimed the kingdom of God and taught about the Lord Jesus Christ—with all boldness and without hindrance! (Acts 28:30–31)

In one sense, the Book of Acts has no end because the proclamation of the gospel continues to this day. The concentric ripples continue to expand out into the world.

It is not clear from the description found in Luke's text in Acts 1 if James was present at the ascension. There are contextual grounds to believe that he was. But it is well worth noting that James certainly was present with the apostles as they awaited the coming of the promised Holy Spirit.

> Then the apostles returned to Jerusalem from the hill called the Mount of Olives, a Sabbath day's walk from the city. When they arrived, they went upstairs to the room where they were staying. Those present were Peter, John, James and Andrew; Philip and Thomas, Bartholomew and Matthew; James son of Alphaeus and Simon the Zealot, and Judas son of James. They all joined together constantly in prayer, along with the women and Mary the mother of Jesus, and with his brothers. (Acts 1:12–14)

The phrase, "*Mary the mother of Jesus, and with his brothers*" must refer to the same brothers that are listed in the gospels, namely, James,

Joseph, Judas (Jude), and Simon.[63] Regent University Professor Jon Mark Ruthven in his introduction to the Epistle of James fully supports this view:

> James apparently was an unbeliever during the ministry
> of Jesus (John 7:3–5). A post-resurrection appearance
> of Christ to him (1 Corinthians 15:7) probably led to
> his conversion, for he is numbered with the believers
> in Acts 1:14.[64]

The family reconciliation that Jesus undertook following his resurrection must have borne fruit. The unbelieving brothers are now numbered among the believers, and the divided family is now reunited. At last, the house of Joseph has rallied round Mary's firstborn son. The occurrence of such a profound reversal lends credibility to the resurrection. It would take a miracle to change the hard-headed James—and a miracle of the highest order is precisely what occurred. The resurrection changed everything.

In the wake of the resurrection, there are two pivotal events in the Book of Acts. The first is the coming of the Holy Spirit on the day of Pentecost. The second is the breakthrough of the gospel messages into the Gentile world. Both events are totally transformational and continue to have a momentous impact right up to the present day.

The first event prefigures and is predictive of the second event. On the day of Pentecost, the Holy Spirit descended upon 120 believers gathered in an upper room in Jerusalem. The primary evidence of the Spirit's arrival was a phenomenon commonly called speaking in tongues.

> When the day of Pentecost came, they were all together
> in one place. Suddenly a Resound like the blowing of
> a violent wind came from heaven and filled the whole
> house where they were sitting. They saw what seemed

---

[63] Matthew 13:55, Mark 6:3.

[64] John Mark Ruthven, "Introduction: The Epistle of James," *Spirit Filled Life Bible, New King James Version,* General Editor Jack W. Hayford, (Thomas Nelson, 1991), p. 1893.

to be tongues of fire that separated and came to rest on each of them. All of them were filled with the Holy Spirit and began to speak in other tongues as the Spirit enabled them.

Now there were staying in Jerusalem God-fearing Jews from every nation under heaven. When they heard this sound, a crowd came together in bewilderment, because each one heard their own language being spoken. Utterly amazed, they asked: "Aren't all these who are speaking Galileans? Then how is it that each of us hears them in our native language? Parthians, Medes and Elamites; residents of Mesopotamia, Judea and Cappadocia, Pontus and Asia, Phrygia and Pamphylia, Egypt and the parts of Libya near Cyrene; visitors from Rome (both Jews and converts to Judaism); Cretans and Arabs—we hear them declaring the wonders of God in our own tongues!" Amazed and perplexed, they asked one another, "What does this mean?"

Some, however, made fun of them and said, "They have had too much wine." (Acts 2:1–13)

Though not all utterances in tongues are understood by those of foreign tongue, in this instance they were. To their astonishment, the pilgrims who arrived in Jerusalem for this Jewish festival heard these Galilean followers of Christ speaking in their native language. The significance of this linguistic breakthrough had them all perplexed, hence the question, "*What does this mean?*"

The apostle Peter stepped forward to address this question. What followed was a succinct explanation of this spiritual phenomenon, which links the Holy Spirit's coming with the ancient prophecy of Joel. According to Peter, in these last days, God's Spirit was being poured out on all people, "*And everyone who calls on the name of the Lord will be saved*" (Acts 2:21).

Peter goes on to explain that this salvation was available through faith in Jesus, who had been crucified, but had risen from the dead. Peter and those assembled with him were witnesses of these things. Furthermore, God signaled his approval of Christ's bodily sacrifice by raising him from the dead and then pouring out the Holy Spirit on his followers.

> "Therefore let all Israel be assured of this: God has made this Jesus, whom you crucified, both Lord and Messiah."
>
> When the people heard this, they were cut to the heart and said to Peter and the other apostles, "Brothers, what shall we do?"
>
> Peter replied, "Repent and be baptized, every one of you, in the name of Jesus Christ for the forgiveness of your sins. And you will receive the gift of the Holy Spirit. The promise is for you and your children and for all who are far off—for all whom the Lord our God will call."
>
> With many other words he warned them; and he pleaded with them, "Save yourselves from this corrupt generation." Those who accepted his message were baptized, and about three thousand were added to their number that day. (Acts 2:36–41)

What we have described here is the birth of the church. On her birthday she grew from one hundred twenty souls to three thousand souls. God was at work among his people.

It should be noted that these new believers were Jewish converts to what is now called Christianity. The term 'Christianity' had not yet been invented. But, already, there was a distinct foreshadowing about what was about to come. The assembled believers spoke in tongues—tongues that were understood by foreigners. Surely this was a portent—a sign that the gospel message was poised to break through into the Gentile world.

In the spirit realm a door had opened to the Gentile world—and it just so happened that James, the brother of Jesus, was the hinge on which this door would swing wide. He would play the pivotal role in the opening of the church to the world.

However, at this early juncture in the Book of Acts and the birth of the church, there is no indication that James would play a leadership role. Why would he? He had not been a follower of the Lord during his earthly ministry. The leadership within Christ's apostolic band had been forged during three and a half years of miracle-filled itinerant ministry. Jesus' inner circle consisted of three men: Peter and the brothers James and John, the sons of Zebedee, whom Jesus nicknamed "*the sons of thunder*" (Mark 3:17). Peter was clearly preeminent among the Twelve and acted as the spokesman for the group, even as he did on the day of Pentecost. James the son of Joseph was a complete outsider to this apostolic group.

But Acts gives us some strong indications that James soon rose to prominence in the church. The narrative structure of Acts records the gospel message spiraling out from Jerusalem to the world. The two central players in the drama that unfolds are first Peter and later Paul, but throughout the book James plays an important background role. He is the *éminence grise* in the story—a respected authority figure to whom others are accountable.

The first indication of this prominent role can be found in the account of Peter's imprisonment in Acts chapter twelve. At this juncture, the persecution of the fledgling church by the Jewish authorities has been sharply intensified. After the martyrdom of Stephen in chapter seven, Saul (Paul) unleashes a round of murderous persecution that sends most of the believers fleeing from the city.[65] A second round of persecution is described in Acts chapter twelve.

> It was about this time that King Herod arrested some who belonged to the church, intending to persecute them. He had James, the brother of John, put to death with the sword. When he saw that this met with approval among the Jews, he proceeded to seize Peter also. This happened during the Festival of Unleavened Bread. After arresting him, he put him in prison, handing him

---

[65] "*On that day a great persecution broke out against the church in Jerusalem, and all except the apostles were scattered throughout Judea and Samaria*" (Acts 8:1).

over to be guarded by four squads of four soldiers each. Herod intended to bring him out for public trial after the Passover.

So Peter was kept in prison, but the church was earnestly praying to God for him. (Acts 12:1–5)

Peter is miraculously freed by an angel who wakes him in the middle of the night and escorts him past the sleeping guards and out through the prison gate, which opens of its own accord. He disrupts the prayer meeting that has been summoned to pray for his release.

But Peter kept on knocking, and when they opened the door and saw him, they were astonished. Peter motioned with his hand for them to be quiet and described how the Lord had brought him out of prison. "Tell James and the other brothers and sisters about this," he said, and then he left for another place. (Acts 12:16–17)

Without doubt, the James that Peter speaks of here is James, the half-brother of Jesus. Bible commentators agree on the identity of the James referred to here. But why would James be accorded this level of respect by Peter? Peter's request implies a degree of accountability to James, as though James held a leadership role. At the very least, Peter sees James as a respected friend and brother in the faith.

I. Howard Marshall in his commentary on this passage states the following:

The James mentioned here is the brother of Jesus (Mk. 6:3) who later figured as the leader of the church in Jerusalem (Acts 15:13, 21:18); Paul regarded him, along with Peter and John, as one of the three 'pillars of the church' (Gal. 2:9). He had been a witness of a resurrection appearance of Jesus (1Cor. 15:7), and hence Paul recognized him as an apostle (Gal. 1:19). It seems probable that from an early stage he was one of the leaders in the church, and at some point he took Peter's place as the recognized leader. The present passage [Acts 12:16–17] need not express more than that he was Peter's deputy at this stage.[66]

Other commentators see James in a leadership role over Peter. George E. Ladd is among the theologians who hold this view. In his comments on Acts 12:16–17, he states the following:

> James, the brother of Jesus, had become the acting head of the Jerusalem church, but he was not with the assembled church at this time. The brethren [other brothers and sisters] may be the elders of [Acts] 11:30 who shared the rule of the church with James.[67]

At this point in the Acts narrative, it may be unclear whether James was Peter's deputy, a coequal or Peter's superior; however, three chapters later it becomes obvious who has the greater authority. In Acts chapter fifteen it becomes apparent that James, the brother of Jesus, is the chief executive officer of the first century church. He makes what is arguably one of the most pivotal decisions in human history—a decision that has profound ramifications even today. He decides that his brother's gospel message will not be confined to Jewry but will spread to the entire world.

---

[66] I. Howard Marshall, *The Acts of the Apostles—Tyndale New Testament Commentaries* (Eerdmans, 1980), pp. 210–211.

[67] George E. Ladd, *The Wycliffe Bible Commentary,* Editors Charles F. Pfeiffer and Everett F. Harrison (Moody, 1972), p. 1146.

---— 11 ——---

The Door of Faith Blows Open

The persecution of the early Christians initiated by Saul (Paul) after the martyrdom of Stephen[68] had an unintended effect. As believers fled for their lives, the gospel message spread out from Jerusalem.

> On that day a great persecution broke out against the church in Jerusalem, and all except the apostles were scattered throughout Judea and Samaria. Godly men buried Stephen and mourned deeply for him. But Saul began to destroy the church. Going from house to house, he dragged off both men and women and put them in prison.
>
> Those who had been scattered preached the word wherever they went. (Acts 8:1b–4)

Acts chapter eight describes the conversion of the Samaritans through the ministry of Philip the evangelist. This brought the Christian message beyond the tight bounds of Jewish faith and lineage. The Samaritans were considered outsiders to the Abrahamic covenant, though some might legitimately claim a partial Jewish heritage as W. Haskell describes.

---

[68] See Acts 7:54–60.

The Samaritans were a mixed race with a heathen core (Ezra 4:2). Their blood would become more and more Hebraized by the addition of renegade Jews and by the intermarriage with surrounding Israelites, who would find among them the familiar worship of former times.[69]

It should be noted that the Samaritans were monotheists. They had their own version of the Pentateuch and believed that Mount Gizrim rather than Jerusalem was the holy place chosen by God. For the purists among the Jewish Christians, the inclusion of Samaritan believers undoubtedly challenged long-held perspectives and conventions. However, the apostles appeared to welcome the news of Samaria's turn toward faith in Jesus Christ.

When the apostles in Jerusalem heard that Samaria had accepted the word of God, they sent Peter and John to Samaria. When they arrived, they prayed for the new believers there that they might receive the Holy Spirit, because the Holy Spirit had not yet come on any of them; they had simply been baptized in the name of the Lord Jesus. Then Peter and John placed their hands on them, and they received the Holy Spirit. (Acts 8:14–17)

If there were any misgivings about welcoming the Samaritans into the Christian fold, they are not recorded in this account. Undoubtedly, Peter and John recognized that this spiritual harvest among the Samaritans was a sovereign work of the Holy Spirit. In all likelihood, they also recalled Jesus' ministry among the Samaritans was marked by kindness and sympathy rather than by the shunning and hostility, which was the societal norm during this time.[70] Nonetheless, it must be noted that with the conversion of the Samaritans, the gospel mes-

[69] W. Haskell, *Unger's Bible Dictionary*, Editor Merrill F. Unger (Moody, 1972), p. 958.
[70] See Luke 10:25–37, Luke 17:11–19, John 4:4–42.

sage had leaped across a significant religious and social barrier. But there was more to come.

Acts chapter eight concludes with the conversion of an Ethiopian eunuch, *"an important official in charge of all the treasury of the Kandake (which means "queen of the Ethiopians")"* (Acts 8:27). This eunuch appears to have been either a convert to Judaism or perhaps a member of the Jewish faith who could trace his lineage back to the time of Solomon. In either case he is identified as an Ethiopian, a man coming from the upper Nile region, possibly Nubia.

Though not explicitly stated, the eunuch was a man of a different race. Apparently Luke, the Gentile author of the Book of Acts, included this account of the Ethiopian's conversion to signal the gospel's leap across a racial barrier. It is well worth noting that the Coptic Church in Ethiopia traces its origin to this account in Acts chapter eight.

The spread of the Christian faith beyond Jerusalem drew a vicious response from Saul (Paul). He was not content to lay waste to the church in Jerusalem. He intended to wipe out the Christian faith wherever he found it.

> Meanwhile, Saul was still breathing out murderous threats against the Lord's disciples. He went to the high priest and asked him for letters to the synagogues in Damascus, so that if he found any there who belonged to the Way, whether men or women, he might take them as prisoners to Jerusalem. As he neared Damascus on his journey, suddenly a light from heaven flashed around him. He fell to the ground and heard a voice say to him, "Saul, Saul, why do you persecute me?"
>
> "Who are you, Lord?" Saul asked.
>
> "I am Jesus, whom you are persecuting," he replied. "Now get up and go into the city, and you will be told what you must do." (Acts 9:1–6)

Saul's miraculous conversion set the early church on a radically different trajectory. Many theologians and biblical scholars see the conversion of Saul of Tarsus as the starting point for the Gentile tidal wave that would flood into the church. They see Saul, who is renamed Paul, as the prima facia cause for the rapid growth of the Christian faith in the Gentile world. However, a closer examination of the Acts narrative and church history reveals that Paul was part of a much larger movement—a Holy Spirit directed movement that propelled the growing church from its cradle in Jerusalem to the ends of the earth. This movement began with Peter not Paul, and it was validated by James.

Acts chapter ten is of pivotal significance in this regard. With Saul's fierce persecution brought to a sudden end by his conversion, we are told that:

> Then the church throughout Judea, Galilee and Sa-
> maria enjoyed a time of peace and was strengthened.
> Living in the fear of the Lord and encouraged by the
> Holy Spirit, it increased in numbers. (Acts 9:31)

However, this increase was confined to Jewish and Samaritan converts to the faith. But as Peter toured through this region performing at least two miraculous signs,[71] he eventually came to sojourn in Joppa at the home of a tanner named Simon. At Joppa the gospel message made a startling leap across the barrier between Jews and uncircumcised Gentiles.

An angel was sent to the household of Cornelius, a Roman centurion.

> One day at about three in the afternoon he had a vi-
> sion. He distinctly saw an angel of God, who came to
> him and said, "Cornelius!"
> Cornelius stared at him in fear. "What is it, Lord?"
> he asked.
> The angel answered, "Your prayers and gifts to the
> poor have come up as a memorial offering before God.

---

[71] At Lydda, Peter healed a paralytic named Aeneas, and at Joppa he raised Dorcas (Tabitha) from the dead. See Acts 9:32–42.

Now send men to Joppa to bring back a man named
Simon who is called Peter. He is staying with Simon
the tanner, whose house is by the sea." (Acts 10:3–6)

The next day as Peter was waiting for his noonday meal to be prepared, he fell into trance in which he saw a sheet lowered from heaven
containing all manner of animals, birds, and reptiles.

Then a voice told him, "Get up, Peter. Kill and eat."
"Surely not, Lord!" Peter replied. "I have never eat-
en anything impure or unclean."
The voice spoke to him a second time, "Do not call
anything impure that God has made clean."
This happened three times, and immediately the
sheet was taken back to heaven. (Acts 10:13–16)

While Peter was still wondering about the meaning of this vision,
three messengers from Cornelius arrived at the door. Peter, who was
keenly attuned to the voice of the Lord, heard the Holy Spirit say, "*Simon, three men are looking for you. So get up and go downstairs. Do not
hesitate to go with them, for I have sent them.*" (Acts 10:19–20)

These events were preparing Peter's heart and mind for the dramatic
shift in direction that the proclamation of the gospel was about to take.
Peter was being sent by the Spirit to a different audience—a Gentile
audience outside the covenantal laws of the Jewish people.

In this regard, even Peter's sojourn in the home of Simon the tanner can be viewed as a preparatory step. Because leather tanners were
required to work with the carcasses of animals their work was considered unclean by many in the Jewish community. As I. Howard Marshall
writes, "Commentators have noted that the tanner's occupation was an
unclean one, and that a person with Pharisaic scruples would avoid contact with such a man."[72]

One could assume that Peter's scruples regarding what was ceremo-
nially clean and unclean were in a state of transition. He certainly did

---

[72] Marshall, *The Acts of the Apostles*, p. 180.

not adhere strictly to the Pharisaic scruples, which went beyond the law and were admired by some first-century Jews.

In this respect he was following the example of his master Jesus, who frequently came into conflict with the Pharisees on such matters.[73]

But stepping into a Gentile's home was a line few observant Jews would deign to cross. Therefore, on the following day when Peter enters Cornelius's home, he offers the following explanation:

> While talking with him [Cornelius], Peter went inside and found a large gathering of people. He said to them: "You are well aware that it is against our law for a Jew to associate with or visit a Gentile. But God has shown me that I should not call anyone impure or unclean. So when I was sent for, I came without raising any objection. May I ask why you sent for me?" (Acts 10:27–29)

In response Cornelius recounts the visitation of the angel, and how he was instructed to send for Peter. The assembled listeners are eager to hear what Peter has to tell them. Of course, Peter uses this heaven-sent opportunity to preach the good news about the ministry of Jesus Christ and his death, burial, and resurrection. He prefaces his message with these words of self-reflection: *"I now realize how true it is that God does not show favoritism but accepts from every nation the one who fears him and does what is right"* (Acts 10:34–35).

It is evident from Peter's remarks that he did not cross this cultural barrier without due consideration and soul searching. Undoubtedly, he knew he would face criticism from fellow Jewish Christians. They would certainly question his decision to enter a Gentile's home. In this single act of hospitality, centuries of rabbinical teaching and practice were being set aside. Many would see this as a grave offence, especially since Peter was a leader in the church.

But this exercise in cross-cultural outreach was not initiated by Peter, Cornelius, or any other man. It was initiated by God. The proof

---

[73] See Matthew 23, Mark 3:23–28, Mark 7:1–23.

of this can be seen in the response to Peter's message. The Holy Spirit intervened while he is still presenting the message. Peter said:

> "All the prophets testify about him [Jesus] that everyone who believes in him receives forgiveness of sins through his name."
>
> While Peter was still speaking these words, the Holy Spirit came on all who heard the message. The circumcised believers who had come with Peter were astonished that the gift of the Holy Spirit had been poured out even on Gentiles. For they heard them speaking in tongues and praising God.
>
> Then Peter said, "Surely no one can stand in the way of their being baptized with water. They have received the Holy Spirit just as we have." So he ordered that they be baptized in the name of Jesus Christ. Then they asked Peter to stay with them for a few days. (Acts 10:43–48)

This event at the home of a Roman centurion in Caesarea has enormous historic significance. It represents the first penetration of the gospel message into the Roman world. Rome was the dominant political and cultural power at that time. This humble home meeting represents the beachhead from which the gospel would spread across Rome's far-flung empire. This was the birthplace of the Gentile church, and Peter played the role of attendant physician to this miraculous birth.

But it was not a birth without controversy. Peter was called to account for his actions that day in Caesarea.

> The apostles and the believers throughout Judea heard that the Gentiles also had received the word of God. So when Peter went up to Jerusalem, the circumcised believers criticized him and said, "You went into the house of uncircumcised men and ate with them." (Acts 11:1–3)

Evidently, many Jewish believers found Peter's actions offensive. They certainly were contrary to the norms proscribed by the teachings of rabbinic Judaism. They felt this breech of the Talmudic law needed to be repaired. Peter must be confronted about his transgression.

In response, Peter provides a full recount of the events leading to his visit to the centurion's home and the subsequent conversion of all who were gathered there. In his justification for his action, he points the finger directly at the Holy Spirit.

> "As I began to speak, the Holy Spirit came on them as he had come on us at the beginning. Then I remembered what the Lord had said: 'John baptized with water, but you will be baptized with the Holy Spirit.' So if God gave them the same gift he gave us who believed in the Lord Jesus Christ, who was I to think that I could stand in God's way?" (Acts 11:15)

What was this *"same gift"* to which Peter refers? Of course, he is referring to speaking in tongues, as happened initially on the day of Pentecost about eleven years prior to Peter's meeting at the home of Cornelius.[74] Peter was struck that without specific instruction on this matter, the same phenomena manifested among these Gentile listeners. While listening to Peter's message, these Gentile hearers became Gentile believers, and the Holy Spirit confirmed their faith by granting them the same gift that the apostles received at Pentecost.

To the consternation of many, the Holy Spirit was making no distinction between Jews and Gentiles. Nonetheless, Peter's explanation appeared to satisfy those who raised objections.

> When they heard this, they had no further objections and praised God, saying, "So then, even to Gentiles

---

[74] The scholars associated with *The International Inductive Study New Testament* situate the Acts 2 day of Pentecost as occurring in 30 AD and the incident at the home of Cornelius as happening in 41 AD. From K. Arthur, *The International Inductive Study New Testament* (Harvest House, 1993), pp. 167, 168, 181.

God has granted repentance that leads to life." (Acts 11:18)

Where was James in this debate? Was he presiding over this interrogation? Luke's account gives us no indication, but it's not difficult to imagine James as one of the first to raise objections to Peter's conduct. Due to his prominent role in the early church, he likely was present to hear Peter's defence. In his epistle penned many years later, James appears to be a rigorous defender of doing things right—correct and by the book. One can easily see how crossing the line into forbidden territory, as Peter had done, would not sit well with James. Nevertheless, Peter was not sanctioned for his conduct. On the contrary, his testimony on this matter led to rejoicing.

One should not assume that the inclusion of Gentile believers within the church proceeded without tension. Centuries of belief, practice, and prejudice are not easily set aside. While many Jewish followers of Christ embraced the message of his sacrificial death and resurrection, it does not logically follow that they would set aside all aspects of their Jewish heritage. They quite rightly saw Jesus as their promised Messiah, but it does not necessarily follow that they saw Jesus as the Savior of the whole world—the Gentile world.

There are an abundance of Old Testament scriptures that point to the salvation of the Gentiles.[75] One can rightly argue, as Paul does, that the salvation of the Gentiles is an integral part of the Abrahamic covenant.[76] But it's one thing to read these prophecies and give mental assent; it's quite a different matter when one sees these things being fulfilled before one's eyes. A complete paradigm shift is required. Undoubtedly some readily embraced this change, while other Jewish believers in Jesus found it difficult or impossible.

Jesus alluded to this in one of his teachings:

---

[75] See Psalm 22:27, Psalm 86:9, Isaiah 9:2, Isaiah 49:6, Isaiah 60:3, Daniel 7:4, Hosea 2:23.

[76] *"This mystery is that through the gospel the Gentiles are heirs together with Israel, members together of one body, and sharers together in the promise in Christ Jesus"* (Ephesians 3:6). See also Genesis 22:18.

"No one sews a patch of unshrunk cloth on an old garment. Otherwise, the new piece will pull away from the old, making the tear worse. And no one pours new wine into old wineskins. Otherwise, the wine will burst the skins, and both the wine and the wineskins will be ruined. No, they pour new wine into new wineskins." (Mark 2:21–22)

New truths are most easily adopted by those who are new to the gospel message. Those trained and hardened in traditional teachings often find it difficult or impossible to embrace radically different ideas or new concepts. Their wineskins have hardened. Accepting Gentiles into the faith required a radical shift in thinking for many Jewish followers of Christ, including the Lord's own disciples. This was true despite his explicit teaching that the gospel was for all—for the whole world.[77]

The acceptance of Cornelius and the converts at his home into the church signals the tacit acceptance that their conversion was the fulfillment of the words of the prophets. However, this welcome into the fold does not answer the question of how these new converts should live. Should they be required to adhere to all the rigours of Judaic law? In their daily lives are they to live as Jews, as Gentile believers in the Jewish Christ, or some blend of the two? Should their males be circumcised? Should they celebrate the Sabbath? Which day should be set aside for worship?

These matters would come to the fore later in the Book of Acts. To some extent, these questions are matters of debate, and even some contention in the broader church today. For example, how should Christians apply Old Testament teachings today? What eventually pushed these questions to the fore in the first century was the robust growth of the church among the Gentiles. We read of this expansion later in the same chapter of Acts:

Now those who had been scattered by the persecution that broke out when Stephen was killed traveled as far

---

[77] See Matthew 24:14, Matthew 28:19, Mark 13:10, Mark 16:15, Luke 24:47, Acts 1:8.

as Phoenicia, Cyprus and Antioch, spreading the word only among Jews. Some of them, however, men from Cyprus and Cyrene, went to Antioch and began to speak to Greeks also, telling them the good news about the Lord Jesus. The Lord's hand was with them, and a great number of people believed and turned to the Lord. (Acts 11:19–21)

This great ingathering resulted in an equally great need for sound teaching in the faith, as well as apostolic oversight. Therefore, the church in Jerusalem responded.

News of this reached the church in Jerusalem, and they sent Barnabas to Antioch. When he arrived and saw what the grace of God had done, he was glad and encouraged them all to remain true to the Lord with all their hearts. He was a good man, full of the Holy Spirit and faith, and a great number of people were brought to the Lord.

Then Barnabas went to Tarsus to look for Saul, and when he found him, he brought him to Antioch. So for a whole year Barnabas and Saul met with the church and taught great numbers of people. The disciples were called Christians first at Antioch. (Acts 11:22–26)

Why was Barnabas chosen to head this mission to Antioch? When Samaria turned to the Lord in Acts chapter eight, it was Peter and John who were sent to investigate and provide further instruction.[78] Why were they not sent to Antioch, since previously they had been engaged in a similar assignment? Luke's account in the Book of Acts provides us with no further details. Perhaps they were fully engaged in other matters of ministry. It is worth noting however that Barnabas was originally from Cyprus (Acts 4:36), and it was men from Cyprus who first brought the gospel to Antioch. For cultural reasons Barnabas may have been a natural choice. He

---

[78] See Acts 8:14–25.

may also have been personally acquainted with these men from Cyprus, thus adding to his appeal as a candidate for this assignment.

Finally, it appears that this was a group decision. We read "*they sent Barnabas to Antioch.*" The Greek used here is plural. It appears that the apostolic leadership within the church decided the matter. It was not decided by one man alone. Was James a part of the decision-making process? From later references in Acts chapter twelve and fifteen, it would seem logical to believe so, though in this instance nothing is stated definitively.

The rapid growth of the Gentile church in Antioch and Paul's arrival there begins a transition within the Book of Acts. Up to this point Peter has been the main character in the narrative, but from this juncture forward Paul assumes the role of the main character. After Peter's imprisonment and miraculous release in chapter twelve, he plays only a minor part in the remainder of the book.

One should not assume that Peter's ministry was diminished, while Paul's excelled. Instead, this transition within the Acts narrative largely reflects the experience and perspective of Luke, the book's author. Luke was Paul's personal doctor and a companion on his missionary journeys.[79] Furthermore, Luke was a Gentile, so the explosive growth of the Gentile church was quite naturally of particular interest to him.

In many respects, Luke played the role of Paul's personal publicist. He ensured that Paul's struggles and triumphs were recorded for posterity. None of the other apostles had a publicist, someone who acted as their press secretary. The inclusion of the Book of Acts in the canon of scripture guaranteed that Christians would be forever reminded about the exploits of the apostle Paul. Undoubtedly, the other apostles accomplished similar feats. Some are heralded in legend, but because these miracles and exploits were not recorded in scripture, memory of them has faded or vanished with the passage of time.[80]

Acts chapters thirteen and fourteen continue the narrative of the Church's explosive growth among the Gentiles. A time of worship,

---

[79] See Colossians 4:14, 2 Timothy 4:11, Philemon 24.

[80] For a detailed examination of the historical evidence regarding the mission and exploits of Christ's original twelve apostles visit: www.biblepath.com/apostles.html.

fasting, and prayer at the church in Antioch sets in motion a chain of events that would rock the Roman Empire.

> Now in the church at Antioch there were prophets and teachers: Barnabas, Simeon called Niger, Lucius of Cyrene, Manaen (who had been brought up with Herod the tetrarch) and Saul. While they were worshiping the Lord and fasting, the Holy Spirit said, "Set apart for me Barnabas and Saul for the work to which I have called them." So after they had fasted and prayed, they placed their hands on them and sent them off. (Acts 13:1–3)

What was this work to which Barnabas and Saul (Paul) had been called? No direct answer is provided in the text, but from the actions and events that follow, it is obvious that these two men are on a mission to bring the gospel message to the Gentiles. This is in full agreement with the word spoken to the disciple Ananias immediately after Saul's encounter with Jesus on the road to Damascus.

> But the Lord said to Ananias, "Go! This man is my chosen instrument to proclaim my name to the Gentiles and their kings and to the people of Israel. I will show him how much he must suffer for my name." (Acts 9:15–16)

Paul is about to begin fulfilling the great purpose for which the Lord has called him to service. Many years later, while speaking in his own defence before King Agrippa, Paul gives this account of his initial encounter with Jesus and the purpose of his calling:

> About noon, King Agrippa, as I was on the road, I saw a light from heaven, brighter than the sun, blazing around me and my companions. We all fell to the ground, and I heard a voice saying to me in Aramaic,

"Saul, Saul, why do you persecute me? It is hard for you to kick against the goads."

Then I asked, "Who are you, Lord?"

"I am Jesus, whom you are persecuting," the Lord replied. "Now get up and stand on your feet. I have appeared to you to appoint you as a servant and as a witness of what you have seen and will see of me. I will rescue you from your own people and from the Gentiles. I am sending you to them to open their eyes and turn them from darkness to light, and from the power of Satan to God, so that they may receive forgiveness of sins and a place among those who are sanctified by faith in me."

"So then, King Agrippa, I was not disobedient to the vision from heaven. First to those in Damascus, then to those in Jerusalem and in all Judea, and then to the Gentiles, I preached that they should repent and turn to God and demonstrate their repentance by their deeds. That is why some Jews seized me in the temple courts and tried to kill me. But God has helped me to this very day; so I stand here and testify to small and great alike. I am saying nothing beyond what the prophets and Moses said would happen—that the Messiah would suffer and, as the first to rise from the dead, would bring the message of light to his own people and to the Gentiles." (Acts 26:13–23)

It is evident from Paul's testimony that he sees his calling as bringing the gospel of Christ to the Gentiles. The prayer meeting in Antioch set him on a course to fulfill his life's mission. Barnabas and Paul began their first missionary journey with a trip to Cyprus. Cyprus was the point of origin for the explosive church growth now evident in the Syrian city of Antioch, and furthermore it was home turf for Barnabas. Undoubtedly, he had many contacts on the island.

A pattern quickly begins to emerge in their ministry on this first journey, first in Cyprus and later in the regions of Pisidia and Lycaonia. They would begin by proclaiming the gospel message in the Jewish synagogues. Their message eventually meets with stiff resistance from many of the Jewish leaders in the community—however, the gospel is received with joy by many of the Gentiles who embrace it with much gratitude.

Often the proclamation of the gospel is accompanied by signs and wonders. On the island of Cyprus, Elymas is struck blind for resisting the gospel (Acts 13:6–12). In Iconium, *"Paul and Barnabas spent considerable time there, speaking boldly for the Lord, who confirmed the message of his grace by enabling them to do miraculous signs and wonders"* (Acts 14:3). In Lystra, with a single command Paul brought healing to a man who was unable to walk from birth (Acts 14:8–10). Undoubtedly, many believed their message because God confirmed the truth of the apostles' words by the miracles that accompanied the gospel's proclamation.

Eventually, persecution becomes acute to the point where Paul and Barnabas' lives are at risk. So, as a result, the apostles move on to virgin territory with their message, where the pattern is repeated yet again. It is worth noting that, according to Luke, persecution and resistance to the message comes largely from the Jews rather than from the Gentile population.[81]

Finally, Paul and Barnabas retrace their steps passing through the towns where they have already ministered.

> They preached the gospel in that city [Derbe] and won a large number of disciples. Then they returned to Lystra, Iconium and Antioch, strengthening the disciples and encouraging them to remain true to the faith. "We must go through many hardships to enter the kingdom of God," they said. Paul and Barnabas appointed elders for them in each church and, with prayer and fasting, committed them to the Lord, in whom they had put their trust. After going through Pisidia, they came into

---

[81] See Acts 13:6–8, Acts 13:44–52; Acts 14:2–7; Acts 14:19–20

Pamphylia, and when they had preached the word in
Perga, they went down to Attalia. (Acts 14:21–25)

The appointment of leaders was of great importance because it ensured the continuance of the church after the apostles' departure. This
tried and proven pattern of ministry was repeated in Paul's subsequent
missionary journeys.

Having achieved tremendous success in their mission despite fierce
opposition, Paul and Barnabas return to Antioch in Syria.

> From Attalia they sailed back to Antioch, where they
> had been committed to the grace of God for the work
> they had now completed. On arriving there, they gath-
> ered the church together and reported all that God had
> done through them and how he had opened a door of
> faith to the Gentiles. And they stayed there a long time
> with the disciples. (Acts 14:26–28)

It was the success of Paul and Barnabas in bringing the gospel to
the Gentiles that precipitated the next great controversy in the church.
The wind of the Spirit had blown the "*door of faith to the Gentiles*" (Acts
14:27) wide open, but there were those in the church who were determined to shut that door—and lock it permanently.

What position would James take in this growing controversy?

———— 12 ————

James the Door Hinge for the Gentile World

t this early point in the history of the church, the city of Antioch
served as home base for the Christian faith in the Gentile world.
Luke records that *the disciples were called Christians first at Antioch*" (Acts 11:26). From here through Paul's ministry, the gospel spread
like wildfire. Antioch was the principal cultural and commercial center
in the eastern Mediterranean region. The biblical scholar G. Downey
describes Syrian Antioch in these terms:

> A Hellenistic city in NW Syria (modern Antakya, Tur-
> key), ranking with Rome and Alexandria as one of the
> three greatest cities of the Greco-Roman world, and an
> early center of Christian expansion.[82]

In this great center, Christianity flourished. But the greatest challenge to further growth came from within the Christian community.

> Certain people came down from Judea to Antioch and
> were teaching the believers: "Unless you are circum-
> cised, according to the custom taught by Moses, you

---

[82] G. Downey, "Antioch (Syrian)," *The Interpreter's Dictionary of the Bible, Volume 1*,
Edited by George Arthur Buttrick (Abingdon, 1984), p. 145.

cannot be saved." This brought Paul and Barnabas into sharp dispute and debate with them. So Paul and Barnabas were appointed, along with some other believers, to go up to Jerusalem to see the apostles and elders about this question. (Acts 15:1–2)

This question had enormous ramifications. Were the new Gentile converts to the faith required to live in accordance with laws of Moses in order to be saved? Must they be circumcised? In essence, must they become Jews in order to live as Christians? Was faith in Christ's finished work on the cross sufficient for salvation or were there additional requirements?

Quite rightly, Paul and Barnabas saw this requirement to be circumcised as a direct challenge to their calling and mission, and a threat to the Gentile church. More fundamentally, it undermined the sufficiency of grace, the redemptive power of the cross and the sacrificial atonement through the blood of Jesus. If one is saved through the observance of the law, rather than through faith, why is there any need for Christ's death on the cross? The cross is stripped of its meaning and power.

Later in his letter to the Galatian church, Paul forcefully argues this very point:

> Mark my words! I, Paul, tell you that if you let yourselves be circumcised, Christ will be of no value to you at all. Again I declare to every man who lets himself be circumcised that he is obligated to obey the whole law. You who are trying to be justified by the law have been alienated from Christ; you have fallen away from grace. For through the Spirit we eagerly await by faith the righteousness for which we hope. For in Christ Jesus neither circumcision nor uncircumcision has any value. The only thing that counts is faith expressing itself through love. (Galatians 5:2–6)

Ultimately, this was a question about DNA. The Gentile believers had the wrong DNA. They were not of Abrahamic lineage; therefore, they were outside the divine covenant and by reason of birth alienated from the blessing of God. Circumcision was the means by which believing Gentiles might be incorporated into the family of God. But Paul correctly argues that those who are circumcised are then required to obey the whole Law of Moses. Relying on human effort and obedience to the law nullifies entirely the concept of spiritual rebirth, which comes by faith.

Jesus taught, *"You must be born again"* (John 3:3–21). This requirement of rebirth applied universally to Jews and Gentiles. Furthermore, rebirth is a work of the Holy Spirit not human effort. Rebirth is experienced through faith. It is a gift from God.[83] Through the miracle of the born-again experience, believers are recipients of divine DNA—eternal DNA—indestructible DNA. Why settle for Abrahamic DNA, when through God's son we can become transformed repositories of divine DNA—children of the eternal, living God?

At this early stage in the churches' development, these doctrines may not have been fully formulated, universally accepted, or understood. But rebirth was certainly occurring as demonstrated by the work of the Holy Spirit. One can study the concept of rebirth at great length, but it can remain nothing more than an academic exercise. A transformed life, and the joy, and peace of the Holy Spirit are true marks of rebirth. In the ministry of Paul and the other apostles, there was ample evidence of changed lives as new believers flooded into the church.

But where was James amid this controversy? Some scholars would have us believe that James was in agreement with the teachers who had arrived in Antioch and were urging the believers to be circumcised. Perhaps, they reason, he had sent them, since Paul's letter to the Galatians gives credence to this perspective.[84] Those who take this view do so because they see James as a Jewish legalist insisting on conformance to the Laws of Moses. In addition, they see an enormous rift between Paul and James. However, the text of Acts chapter fifteen does not support this view.

---

[83] *"For it is by grace you have been saved, through faith—and this is not from yourselves, it is the gift of God—not by works, so that no one can boast"* (Ephesians 2:8–9).

[84] *For before certain men came from James, he used to eat with the Gentiles. But when they arrived, he began to draw back and separate himself from the Gentiles because he was afraid of those who belonged to the circumcision group.* (Galatians 2:12)

What becomes plainly evident in Acts 15 is that James is seen as the leader of the church. One cannot read this chapter without concluding just that. Three observations can be made, which prove this point:

- James provides oversight to the church, the body of Christ.
- The leaders in the church are accountable to him.
- He is the one who renders judgement on this issue of paramount importance.

On the first point, it is significant that this synod—or council, as it is often called—took place in Jerusalem. New Testament scholars are generally in agreement that this council took place in about 50 AD.[85] Jerusalem would seem like the logical choice since it was the birthplace of the church, and it certainly flourished there in the early years. But the church had grown and spread out geographically from this home base. Some of this dispersion was due to severe persecution in Jerusalem. Peter fled the city for this very reason; however, James remained.[86]

There is no indication in scripture that Peter returned to reside in Jerusalem. He began what can be described as an itinerant ministry, following in the footsteps of his Lord and Master. Some of that ministry is detailed in the earlier chapters of Acts and from Paul's letter to the Galatians we also know he traveled to Antioch.

On the other hand, it appears that James' ministry was centered in Jerusalem. In the writings of several early church fathers, James is identified as the first Bishop of Jerusalem.[87] Similarly, the Eastern Orthodox Church recognizes James as the first Bishop of Jerusalem.

---

[85] Arthur, *The International Inductive Study New Testament*, p.186.

[86] Acts 12:16–17.

[87] In the late 2nd century, Clement of Alexandria recorded the following: "For they say that Peter and James and John, after the ascension of our savior, as if also preferred by our Lord, strove not after honor, but chose James the Just as bishop of Jerusalem." From Eusebius' *Church History, Book 2:1*, quoting Clement of Alexandria's *Sixth Hypotyposes*, Translated by Arthur Cushman McGiffert. *From Nicene and Post-Nicene Fathers, Second Series, Vol. 1*, Edited by Philip Schaff and Henry Wace (Christian Literature, 1890), Revised and edited for New Advent by Kevin Knight, www.newadvent.org/fathers/250102.htm.

The Clementine Homilies and Clementine Recognitions, which are romances about the life of Clementine[88] dating from the fourth century but partly based on Jewish Christian sources of an earlier time, call James "bishop of bishops." In these writings Peter and the other apostles are accredited by James.[89]

If James was functioning in his role as bishop, was he providing oversight only to the church in Jerusalem or was he providing general oversight to the whole church? This is a question of considerable importance as we examine Acts chapter fifteen.

If Peter was providing general oversight to the church, then it might logically follow that the church leadership would gather to discuss this important matter at Peter's current place of ministry, but this is not the case. Peter appears and testifies at the Jerusalem Council as a delegate—a trusted apostolic delegate. He does not have the final say in the matter being discussed. The final decision is left to James.

Though Luke never personally interjects himself into the Acts account, the way in which he frames the events of chapter fifteen leaves the reader with the impression that he may have accompanied Paul and Barnabas on this journey from Antioch to Jerusalem. It certainly is possible that he was appointed as one of the believers sent as delegates to the council.[90] Since Doctor Luke was a Gentile, this matter certainly would have a huge bearing on his life and faith, and he records the events in some detail. A close examination of his account is warranted.

The church sent them [Paul, Barnabas and 'some believers'] on their way, and as they traveled through Phoenicia and Samaria, they told how the Gentiles had been converted. This news made all the believers very glad.

---

[88] Clementine of Rome died around 100 AD and is believed to be the second or third bishop of Rome.

[89] W. A. Beardslee, "James," *The Interpreter's Dictionary of the Bible, Volume 2*, Edited by George Arthur Buttrick (Abingdon, 1984), p. 793.

[90] See Acts 15:3.

> When they came to Jerusalem, they were welcomed
> by the church and the apostles and elders, to whom
> they reported everything God had done through them.
> (Acts 15:3–4)

Luke then goes on to clearly delineate the question that the council must decide:

> Then some of the believers who belonged to the party
> of the Pharisees stood up and said, "The Gentiles must
> be circumcised and required to keep the law of Moses."
> The apostles and elders met to consider this ques-
> tion. (Acts15:5–6)

Apparently, some Pharisees had come to faith in Christ despite the frequent clashes that had occurred between them during his earthly ministry. Quite naturally some of these Pharisees continued with their hardline requirements of obedience to every jot and tittle of the Law of Moses. At least on the surface, it appears that their adherence to Mosaic Law took precedence over their allegiance to the law of love introduced by Christ.[91]

We are told that after much discussion, Peter addressed the assembled leaders. Undoubtedly, there was rigorous debate on this topic, since it had profound doctrinal implications and had a direct bearing on the outreach mission of the church. Was obedience to the Mosaic Law a requirement for salvation? Was salvation a gift from God received by faith or was it merited through works and religious observances such as circumcision and adherence to sabbath requirements? Were the new Gentile converts genuinely welcome in the church? Was Paul's mission to the Gentile's a valid extension of the ongoing mission of Christ on the earth? All these questions were in play as Peter addressed the synod.

---

[91] *A new command I give you: Love one another. As I have loved you, so you must love one another. By this everyone will know that you are my disciples, if you love one another.* (John 13:34–35)

"Brothers, you know that some time ago God made a choice among you that the Gentiles might hear from my lips the message of the gospel and believe. God, who knows the heart, showed that he accepted them by giving the Holy Spirit to them, just as he did to us. He did not discriminate between us and them, for he purified their hearts by faith. Now then, why do you try to test God by putting on the necks of Gentiles a yoke that neither we nor our ancestors have been able to bear? No! We believe it is through the grace of our Lord Jesus that we are saved, just as they are." (Acts 15:7–11)

Peter's response on this matter is clear and unequivocal. Peter points out that this matter has already been decided—not by man—but by God. God chose to have the message of the gospel preached to the Gentiles. He did so by sending an angel to the home of a Roman centurion named Cornelius. The angel's instructions were to send for Simon Peter, whose heart was prepared in advance through a vision. The gospel message was proclaimed to the Gentiles because God wanted it preached to the Gentiles. He initiated this whole matter.

Moreover, the Gentiles at Cornelius' home responded in faith. They believed the message of the gospel. Peter points out that God "*purified their hearts by faith*" (Acts 15:9). Works or merit based on obedience to the law did not enter into the picture.

Furthermore, God demonstrated that the Gentiles were accepted "*by giving the Holy Spirit to them*" (Acts 15:8). This was apparent "*for they heard them speaking in tongues and praising God*" (Acts 10:46). The Pentecostal experience was visited upon these Gentile believers even as it had initially come to the apostles and the hundred and twenty. God revealed that He had accepted the Gentiles into the household of faith without any preconditions. He made no distinction whatsoever between Jews and Gentiles.

In short, Peter was saying that this was entirely God's doing. God initiated the whole process of bringing the Gentiles into the church, and it was perilous for the church to now place restrictions on the people whom God had so freely and graciously welcomed into the family. Peter calls this testing God. His words bear repeating:

> Now then, why do you try to test God by putting on the necks of Gentiles a yoke that neither we nor our ancestors have been able to bear? No! We believe it is through the grace of our Lord Jesus that we are saved, just as they are. (Acts 15:7–11)

With these words Peter echoes the thoughts and sentiments of Jesus—who, during the week of his arrest, excoriated the Pharisees and teachers of the law.

> The teachers of the law and the Pharisees sit in Moses' seat. So you must be careful to do everything they tell you. But do not do what they do, for they do not practice what they preach. They tie up heavy, cumbersome loads and put them on other people's shoulders, but they themselves are not willing to lift a finger to move them. (Matthew 23:2–4)

Quite rightly Peter was unwilling to impose a burden on the Gentiles that Jesus had spoken against.[92] Instead, Peter embraced the grace of God. By doing this he placed Jews and Gentiles on the same footing. Both are saved by the grace of Jesus Christ and not by works of the law.

In his statement before the Jerusalem Council, Peter encapsulates the great truths of the gospel and points the way forward for the church. Decades later, Paul in his Epistle to the Romans expounds at great length on the truths that Peter has succinctly stated here. Peter simply directs the council's attention to the choices that God has already made. God chose to save both Jews and Gentiles by grace through faith and to pour out His Spirit on them. This was and to this day continues to be His doing and not the work of human effort.

---

[92] See also Luke 11:37–54.

Peter's declaration in favor of grace for the Gentiles rather than the Mosaic Law was followed by the testimony of Paul and Barnabas:

> The whole assembly became silent as they listened to Barnabas and Paul telling about the signs and wonders God had done among the Gentiles through them. (Acts 15:12)

Through their testimony, Barnabas and Paul persuasively reinforced the argument Peter had presented. The conversion of the Gentiles was God's doing. He had initiated it through Peter and now was continuing that work through Barnabas and Paul. The proof of this was in "*the signs and wonders God had done.*" If God was opposed to the inclusion of the Gentiles in the Christian faith, there would be no signs and wonders as the gospel message was presented. Instead, miraculous signs and wonders accompanied the preaching of the gospel, giving it credence. Large numbers of Gentiles believed the message they heard because they witnessed demonstrations of God's power.

Signs and wonders were an integral part of the spread of the gospel as recorded in the Book of Acts.[93] Certainly, the apostles viewed these wonders as a natural extension of Jesus' ministry. According to Mark's Gospel, after his resurrection Jesus predicted this bursting forth of the miraculous:

> Later Jesus appeared to the Eleven as they were eating; he rebuked them for their lack of faith and their stubborn refusal to believe those who had seen him after he had risen.
>
> He said to them, "Go into all the world and preach the gospel to all creation. Whoever believes and is baptized will be saved, but whoever does not believe will be condemned. And these signs will accompany those who believe: In my name they will drive out demons;

---

[93] See Acts 3:7, Acts 5:5 & 10, Acts 5:15, Acts 9:34, Acts 9:40, Acts 13:11, Acts 14:3, Acts 14:10, Acts 19:11–12, Acts 20:10, Acts 28:5, Acts 28:8,

they will speak in new tongues; they will pick up snakes with their hands; and when they drink deadly poison, it will not hurt them at all; they will place their hands on sick people, and they will get well." (Mark 16:14–18)

Furthermore, Jesus had promised his disciples that they would do even greater things than he had done.

Very truly I tell you, whoever believes in me will do the works I have been doing, and they will do even greater things than these, because I am going to the Father. And I will do whatever you ask in my name, so that the Father may be glorified in the Son. You may ask me for anything in my name, and I will do it. (John 14:12–14)

As the apostles heard the testimony of Paul and Barnabas, they undoubtedly harkened back to the words of Jesus. God was at work claiming a people for Himself. The proof of this was in the manifestation of signs and wonders as the gospel was presented to the Gentiles, their positive response to the message, and the demonstrable presence of the Holy Spirit among them.

There are those who see substantial differences between Peter and Paul, but there are none on display here. The core of the gospel message they present is essentially the same: the door to salvation is open to all, Jew and Gentile, by grace through faith alone in the redeeming death and resurrection of Jesus Christ.

Together here at the Jerusalem Council, Peter and Paul present a united front. They act as a tag team delivering the decisive blows that demolished the argument in favor of circumcision and adherence to Mosaic Law. We see them work in cooperation with one another here at the Council and later out on the field.

We know their position carried the day due James' response:

When they finished, James spoke up. "Brothers," he said, "listen to me. Simon [Peter] has described to us how God first intervened to choose a people for his name from the Gentiles. The words of the prophets are in agreement with this, as it is written:

> "'After this I will return and rebuild David's fallen tent.
>
> Its ruins I will rebuild, and I will restore it, that the rest of mankind may seek the Lord, even all the Gentiles who bear my name, says the Lord, who does these things'—things known from long ago.[94]

"It is my judgment, therefore, that we should not make it difficult for the Gentiles who are turning to God. Instead we should write to them, telling them to abstain from food polluted by idols, from sexual immorality, from the meat of strangled animals and from blood. For the law of Moses has been preached in every city from the earliest times and is read in the synagogues on every Sabbath." (Acts 15:13–21)

From this account one clearly has the sense that James is presiding over this gathering or Council. He is providing oversight as the question is framed and opposing arguments are debated. At the conclusion of the debate, James states his position and renders his judgment on the matter. In this regard the Jerusalem Council proceedings resemble a court case with a presiding judge, namely James, pronouncing the final verdict.

There is no indication that this is a democratic assembly where a final vote on the motion is taken. Rather the Council follows the format of a judicial council, where the matter is considered and decided by a judge or overseer. This format was customary in both Jewish and Roman practise during this time and continues in various forms to this day.

In his statement James concurs with Peter's testimony. In essence, he concludes that this is a decision that God has already made. *"Simon has described to us how God first intervened to choose a people for his name from*

---

[94] James is quoting Amos, the Old Testament prophet (Amos 9:11–12).

DAVID KITZ

the Gentiles" (Acts 15:14). He then goes on to reinforce his position by quoting from the prophet Amos.

There are several Old Testament scriptures that predict the Gentiles will turn in faith to the God of Israel. Why did James choose to quote this particular passage?

First and foremost, the Amos passage captures the thought that the entry of the Gentiles into God's kingdom is God's idea. It is the Lord "*who does these things.*" What Peter had described was an intervention of God in bringing the Gentiles at the household of Cornelius to faith. Similarly, Paul and Barnabas described God's intervention by means of signs and wonders as they preached the gospel to the Gentiles on their first missionary journey. So James concludes that the conversion of the Gentiles was God's idea and indeed God's doing.

The phrase "*David's fallen tent*" also merits some consideration. Jesus was a direct descendant from the kingly line of David. James sees God's intervention as restoring the rule of the Davidic dynasty through the eternal reign of King Jesus. As the brother of Jesus, James may well have seen himself as part of that Davidic line extending the kingdom of God on the earth. Again, this is God's doing, and James finds himself in the pivotal role of opening wide the door to the Gentiles.

Having stated his position on the matter, James renders his verdict. "*It is my judgment, therefore, that we should not make it difficult for the Gentiles who are turning to God*" (Acts 15:19). The Greek word *krino* is translated here as judgment. In fact, *krino* is translated as judge or judgment eighty-seven times in the New Testament.[95] Most modern translations render *krino* as judgment; however, the traditional King James Version translates *krino* as *sentence*. "*Wherefore my sentence is, that we trouble not them, which from among the Gentiles are turned to God*" (Acts 15:19). By translating *krino* in this way, the King James translators highlight the magisterial role of James at the Council. He has declared his ruling on the matter.

There can be little doubt that James is viewed as the head of the church by all those present. He fulfills the role of chief executive officer.

---

[95] Robert Young, *Analytical Concordance to the Bible, Index-Lexicon to the New Testament*, Revised by William B. Stevenson (Eerdmans, 1972), p. 78.

136

How do we know this? He has the undisputed final word on this crucial matter of faith, practice, and doctrine.

But one gets the sense that James was not heavy handed or dictatorial in reaching his decision. Through the discussion and a full airing of the matter, he was working to reach a consensus within the church. Evidence for this can be found in the actions that follow his ruling.

> Then the apostles and elders, with the whole church, decided to choose some of their own men and send them to Antioch with Paul and Barnabas. They chose Judas (called Barsabbas) and Silas, men who were leaders among the believers. (Acts 15:22)

There was agreement among the apostles, the elders, and the whole church on this matter.

With his decision James secured the future of the church. Christianity would not remain as an obscure sect within Judaism. It would spread around the world and become a dominant force in world history through the next two millennia. His decision made possible the unhindered progress of the gospel in the Roman Empire and beyond.

James' judgment puts truth to these words, which were sung about his brother Jesus and recorded in John's Revelation:

> And they sang a new song, saying:
> "You are worthy to take the scroll and to open its seals, because you were slain, and with your blood you purchased for God persons from every tribe and language and people and nation.
> You have made them to be a kingdom and priests to serve our God, and they will reign on the earth." (Revelation 5:9–10)

— 13 —

James the Mediator between Two Camps

As the leader of the church, James finds himself straddling the gulf between two factions: the Judaizers who insist that male Gentile coverts to Christianity be circumcised and follow the Mosaic Law, and a faith-oriented faction led by Paul that believes in the sufficiency of grace, apart from adherence to the Law. The struggle between these opposing positions informs a considerable portion of New Testament scripture. Paul's letter to the Galatians focuses almost exclusively on this topic, but this issue or doctrine forms an underlying theme throughout Paul's writing.

At the Jerusalem Council, James comes down decisively on the side of grace and the expansion of the Christian faith into the Gentile world. His ruling clearly endorsed the position taken by Peter and Paul, and he even tempers his remarks by placing some rather minor restrictions on the Gentile converts. Some may view this as a concession to the hardliners in the Jewish faction.

> It is my judgment, therefore, that we should not make it difficult for the Gentiles who are turning to God. Instead we should write to them, telling them to abstain from food polluted by idols, from sexual immorality, from the meat of strangled animals and from blood.

> For the law of Moses has been preached in every city
> from the earliest times and is read in the synagogues on
> every Sabbath. (Acts 15:19–21)

James certainly does not abandon the law entirely. He is not saying, "Believe in Christ and then live as you please." Neither do any of the apostles. In his letter to the Romans, Paul claims he is falsely accused of promoting this errant doctrine.[96] Instead, Paul says faith in Christ prompts conformity to the image Christ, who fulfilled the Law (Colossians 3:9–11). Spiritual rebirth initiates and instills life transformation. Believers are changed by their faith in Christ and drawn to obedience to him. Spiritual DNA expresses itself, even as natural DNA does. The child resembles his natural father. Even so, the character and conduct of the born-again believer should increasingly resemble his heavenly Father and his spiritual brother Jesus Christ.

Paul amplifies this thought in his letter to the Romans:

> For those God foreknew he also predestined to be con-
> formed to the image of his Son, that he might be the
> firstborn among many brothers and sisters. (Romans
> 8:29)

The restrictions or regulations that James places on the Gentile believers appear to be relatively inconsequential, but they had implications for the daily lives of Gentile believers. It was common for meat sold in the Gentile markets to be offered first as an animal sacrifice to idols. This made the Christian consumer of this meat an unwilling participant in pagan idolatry. Clearly this would be offensive to the sensibilities of Jewish believers.

How strictly these regulations were adhered to remains an open question. In the fourteenth chapter of his letter to the Romans Paul discusses this issue of food and abstaining from meat at some length. He also gives these instructions to the believers in Corinth:

---

[96] See Romans 6:1–3.

Eat anything sold in the meat market without raising questions of conscience, for, "The earth is the Lord's, and everything in it."

If an unbeliever invites you to a meal and you want to go, eat whatever is put before you without raising questions of conscience. But if someone says to you, "This has been offered in sacrifice," then do not eat it, both for the sake of the one who told you and for the sake of conscience. I am referring to the other person's conscience, not yours. For why is my freedom being judged by another's conscience? If I take part in the meal with thankfulness, why am I denounced because of something I thank God for?

So whether you eat or drink or whatever you do, do it all for the glory of God. Do not cause anyone to stumble, whether Jews, Greeks or the church of God—even as I try to please everyone in every way. For I am not seeking my own good but the good of many, so that they may be saved. (1 Corinthians 10:25–33)

Similarly, the entire eighth chapter of 1 Corinthians is devoted to this topic. Clearly Paul saw James' injunction against eating meat offered to idols as an issue of considerable importance, or he would not have addressed this topic in his epistles to the church.

Undoubtedly, the advice cited above was given in keeping with Paul's understanding of James' directive in Acts 15. Overall Paul's concern is chiefly that believers keep their conscience pure. He does not see "*food polluted by idols*" as a clear black and white issue, but rather as a matter of the heart or the intent of the believer. Paul implies that food is sanctified if it is received with thanksgiving. In so doing, he is providing a practical interpretation of how believers can keep themselves spiritually pure while living in a pagan world.

The injunction against sexual immorality needs little explanation. The Greco-Roman world was awash in sexual immorality, much of it linked to various fertility cults. Abstinence from sexual immorality also involved a rejection of the shrine prostitutes—both male and female—and ritual orgies linked to the worship of these deities. Clearly there was a strong sense that these new Gentile believers must renounce these practices and forms of worship as they embrace a new lifestyle within the body of Christ.

James' command to abstain *"from the meat of strangled animals and from blood"* stems directly from Levitical law, where God says:

> I will set my face against any Israelite or any foreigner residing among them who eats blood, and I will cut them off from the people. For the life of a creature is in the blood, and I have given it to you to make atonement for yourselves on the altar; it is the blood that makes atonement for one's life. Therefore I say to the Israelites, "None of you may eat blood, nor may any foreigner residing among you eat blood." (Leviticus 17:10–12)

This reference to the foreigner, as cited here, has direct relevance as the Jewish believers contemplate welcoming Gentiles into their fellowship. The fellowship meal has particular significance in Middle Eastern culture. For friendship and fellowship to be sealed, the sharing of a meal together was essential. If this overture to the Gentiles was to be significant and meaningful, then Jewish Christian believers and Gentile Christian believers should be able to sit together and eat a fellowship meal together.

But truly the focal point of their fellowship must be Christ—Christ whose redeeming sacrifice was sealed in blood—Christ Jesus who instituted the Eucharist to commemorate the shedding of his blood. By his blood, atonement was made for both Jews and Gentiles. Their fellowship meals included the celebration of the Eucharist. Evidence of this can be found in Paul's instructions on communion.[97]

Surely the following words had true resonance as James considered the unity of faith between Jews and Gentiles: *"it is the blood that makes*

---

[97] See 1 Corinthians 11:17–34.

atonement for one's life. "His brother's blood was shed to make that atonement possible. True communion centered around the sacrificial shedding of Jesus' blood.

With James having ruled on this matter, the assembly decided to communicate its decision to those most directly affected—the Gentile churches. Their message also makes it clear that those who caused this doctrinal disturbance were not sent or authorized by the apostolic leadership.

> Then the apostles and elders, with the whole church, decided to choose some of their own men and send them to Antioch with Paul and Barnabas. They chose Judas (called Barsabbas) and Silas, men who were leaders among the believers. With them they sent the following letter:
>
> The apostles and elders, your brothers,
>
> To the Gentile believers in Antioch, Syria and Cilicia:
>
> Greetings.
>
> We have heard that some went out from us without our authorization and disturbed you, troubling your minds by what they said. So we all agreed to choose some men and send them to you with our dear friends Barnabas and Paul—men who have risked their lives for the name of our Lord Jesus Christ. Therefore we are sending Judas and Silas to confirm by word of mouth what we are writing. It seemed good to the Holy Spirit and to us not to burden you with anything beyond the following requirements: You are to abstain from food sacrificed to idols, from blood, from the meat of strangled animals and from sexual immorality. You will do well to avoid these things.
>
> Farewell.
>
> So the men were sent off and went down to Antioch, where they gathered the church together and delivered

the letter. The people read it and were glad for its encouraging message. (Acts 15:22–31)

James has decisively sided with Peter and Paul on this critical issue. The gospel of grace as opposed to Jewish legalism has triumphed. For the sake of unity, James has added some conditions onto his sweeping welcome of the Gentile believers. Despite this ruling, some Judaizers will persist in trying to force Gentile converts to be circumcised, but they will lack the authority of the church. A certain tension will remain between the proponents of grace and the proponents of legalism. It is a tension that remains in some form between legalistically-inclined and grace-centered believers to this day. Nevertheless, the message is clear: James has ruled in favor of grace.

By welcoming the Gentile believers into the church, James signaled that he fully grasps the significance of the born-again experience. He has come full circle. He has come fully around to his brother's position, which he so vehemently opposed as a young man—when he gathered the family around him to take charge of Jesus because, by his reasoning, Jesus had gone mad (Mark 3:20–22.).

On that occasion with his family waiting at the door, Jesus responded with these words:

> "Who are my mother and my brothers?" he asked.
> Then he looked at those seated in a circle around him and said, "Here are my mother and my brothers! Whoever does God's will is my brother and sister and mother." (Mark 3:33–35)

According to Jesus' reasoning the spiritual family—spiritual genetics—took precedence over the natural family. Though at the time James rejected his brother and his concept of spiritual rebirth, he now finds himself in full agreement with it. His conversion at the appearance of the risen Christ changed everything.[98] What he rejected as heresy before his own rebirth, he now affirms as gospel truth. James now

---

[98] See 1 Corinthians 15:3–9.

sees the family of believers as his true family—a family that includes even Gentiles.

On a personal level, James was now Jesus' brother in the Spirit as well as in the flesh.

Furthermore, at the Jerusalem Council, James plays the role his brother would have him play. He institutes his brother's will by ensuring that the gospel message was available to all throughout the world, regardless of race or gender. James recognizes that those seated before him, eager to hear the gospel message, are his brothers and sisters. He is acting as a doorkeeper to the kingdom of God. In that role, he is guaranteeing that the door is open to all. Anyone can come and enter through repentance and faith in the shed blood of his brother Jesus.

Without question this was a difficult decision to make. By welcoming the Gentiles, James may have sealed the fate of the Jewish church—the church he led. There was a point when it appeared as though Christianity might become the dominant belief system among the Jews. Then severe persecution hindered its advance. Now, with its doors open to the Gentiles, the legalistic members of the Jewish faith could quickly and easily dismiss the Christian faith as an aberrant heresy, unworthy of consideration. As a result, further church growth among the Jewish community was likely stymied.

Did James know that this would be the outcome of his decision to throw the doors open to Gentiles? He probably had some idea of how this would impede the growth of the church among the Jews in their homeland. He knew the ethos of his people. The hardline Pharisaic viewpoint was popular with many Jews, and a fierce, religiously motivated ethnic pride was even more widespread. Generations of religious indoctrination are not easily set aside. Jesus clashed with it; now James does as well.

Despite this, James chose his brother's will—God's will—not his own. Perhaps he caught a glimpse of the long view—a view that saw the swift rise to prominence of the church in the Greco-Roman world. Perhaps he simply recognized that this was God's doing—a work of the Spirit—not simply the work of man. Whatever the reason, James played a pivotal role in promoting the advance of the gospel and in shaping world history for the next two thousand years. Without him Christianity may well have remained an obscure Jewish sect. He was the hinge—the doorkeeper—and he opened the gospel door to the sea of humanity.

But one question remains. How did James come to play such a prominent role in the early church?

—— 14 ——

Why James?

How and why was James able to play such a preeminent role in the first century church? He was not part of Jesus' roving band of disciples. He was not a witness to Christ's miracles and did not sit under his teaching. Throughout Jesus' earthly ministry James was a critic and an unbeliever.[99] How then could this outsider rise to the role of church leader and adjudicator in matters of policy and doctrine?

Obviously, his post-resurrection encounter with Jesus was transformational in every way. James was changed. He was a new man—a born-again believer. Because of his intimate knowledge of Jesus, he undoubtedly had a unique understanding—a fuller grasp—of the mind of Christ.

According to Christian tradition, James was a deeply devout individual, who was esteemed for his piety.

> According to Hegesippus, writing ca. 180 (quoted by Euseb. Hist. II.23.4–18), James was a Nazirite and spent so much time on his knees in intercession for the people that his knees grew horny like a camel's. He was

---

revered by all as "the Just" (a title perhaps transferred from Christ; cf. Acts 3:14; 7:52; 22:14).[100]

The veracity of this description is hard to determine, but often legendary accounts encapsulate a good deal of truth. It certainly is likely that James was a man of prayer and spiritual ardour, since his epistle reflects and encourages these very characteristics. He calls for holy and righteous conduct with no excuses.

These qualities would have been evident and admired by the twelve apostles. Furthermore, these character traits testify to the dramatic change that occurred in James. Sound moral character and a spirit attuned to God are prerequisites for leadership in the church, and it certainly appears that the James possessed these traits.

Paul's high respect for James is noteworthy. In his epistle to the Galatians, Paul cites his relationship with James as a point of defense against the Judaizers, who insist that Gentile converts must be circumcised.

> Then after three years, I went up to Jerusalem to get acquainted with Cephas [Peter] and stayed with him fifteen days. I saw none of the other apostles—only James, the Lord's brother. I assure you before God that what I am writing you is no lie.
>
> Then I went to Syria and Cilicia. I was personally unknown to the churches of Judea that are in Christ. They only heard the report: "The man who formerly persecuted us is now preaching the faith he once tried to destroy." And they praised God because of me. (Galatians 1:18–24)

The independent-minded Paul insisted that the gospel message as he understood it came directly by revelation from the Lord; nonetheless, he gained insight and affirmation through his early contact with Peter and

---

[100] Beardslee, "James," *The Interpreter's Dictionary of the Bible, Volume 2,* p. 793.

James. He uses this affirmation to bolster his own authority as a bonafide minister of the gospel. It is apparent that Paul accords respect to James because he is *"the Lord's brother,"* a recognized leader in the church, and also an apostle.

The importance of Paul's first meeting with James should not be underestimated. Their spiritual journeys had much in common. Both came from devoutly religious backgrounds. Prior to conversion, both approached their faith from a rigid, legalistic mindset. As young men, both were hostile to Christ and the gospel message, and both had a personal encounter with the resurrected Jesus—a visitation from the Lord. It was an encounter that radically changed the trajectory of their lives.

Imagine for a moment the discussion they had in this first meeting, as each explored the other's personal story. Their lives ran parallel to one another. Both needed a direct encounter—more like a confrontation with Jesus—in order to come to faith and change their ways.[101] Both were unique when compared with the other apostles, in that they needed this direct visitation to change their hostility into adoration. They were special because their calling and mission came via a direct and sudden intervention by Jesus. They were singled out by him.

The significance of James' designation as an apostle should not be overlooked. James, along with Paul and the Twelve, was a witness to the resurrection of Jesus. This included an impartation of apostolic authority to carry out their mission to the church and the world—an authority derived from their meeting with the Lord.

It is logical to conclude that in this first meeting James 'got' Paul. He understood where he was coming from, perhaps more than any other man. Similarly, Paul 'got' James. They shared a mutual and parallel experience that connected them as brothers in the Spirit. This mutual understanding was foundational to their relationship and would stand them in good stead over the years, as their apostolic ministry took them to divergent fields. They both understood that they were called by the

---

[101] For Paul's confrontation with the resurrected Jesus, see Acts 9:1–19. For James' encounter with the resurrected Jesus, see 1 Corinthians 15:3–8.

Lord Jesus to fulfill a specific role or ministry. In Paul's case it was to bring the gospel to the Gentiles.[102]

The question is, did Jesus also give James a specific apostolic assignment when he appeared to him after his resurrection? Did he appoint James as the leader of the church in Jerusalem? Or was this a role that James grew into over time? Did the twelve apostles simply come to recognize the proven leadership qualities that James possessed? Some early Christian literature accords James a pre-eminent leadership role, as W. A. Beardslee explains:

> The Clementine Homilies and Clementine Recognitions, which are romances about the life of Clement dating from the fourth century but partly based on Jewish Christian sources of an earlier time, call James "bishop of bishops." In these writings Peter and the other apostles are accredited by James (Clementine Recognitions IV.35). James is presented as sending out the apostles in the Coptic Gnostic "Letter of James" of the Jung Codex."[103]

There can be no doubt from New Testament sources that James became the recognized authority within in the Jerusalem church, but this was not immediately the case after the church's first Pentecost. Unlike the apocryphal accounts cited above, it would appear that over time James assumed this role and was recognized for it, even as Paul grew into his role as the apostle to the Gentiles. Again, in this respect Paul and James share a similar story. Due to their initial opposition to the gospel, it took years for them to gain the trust of the church, even after their personal encounter with their resurrected Savior. If James had any role in sending out the apostles, it is not recorded in scripture, and it certainly did not happen

---

[102] "But the Lord said to him [Ananais], 'Go, for he [Paul] is an instrument whom I have chosen to bring my name before Gentiles and kings and before the people of Israel; I myself will show him how much he must suffer for the sake of my name.'" (Acts 9:15–16) See also Paul's account of his conversion, Acts 26:15–18.

[103] Beardslee, "James," *The Interpreter's Dictionary of the Bible, Volume 2*, p. 793.

prior to the ingathering initiated by the conversion of the centurion Cornelius in Acts 10.

Returning to the second chapter of Galatians, we see that Paul continues to use his affirmation by James and the apostles to bolster his authority in his argument against trusting in circumcision.

> Then after fourteen years, I went up again to Jerusalem, this time with Barnabas. I took Titus along also. I went in response to a revelation and, meeting privately with those esteemed as leaders; I presented to them the gospel that I preach among the Gentiles. I wanted to be sure I was not running and had not been running my race in vain. Yet not even Titus, who was with me, was compelled to be circumcised, even though he was a Greek. This matter arose because some false believers had infiltrated our ranks to spy on the freedom we have in Christ Jesus and to make us slaves. We did not give in to them for a moment, so that the truth of the gospel might be preserved for you.
>
> As for those who were held in high esteem—whatever they were makes no difference to me; God does not show favoritism—they added nothing to my message. On the contrary, they recognized that I had been entrusted with the task of preaching the gospel to the uncircumcised, just as Peter had been to the circumcised. For God, who was at work in Peter as an apostle to the circumcised, was also at work in me as an apostle to the Gentiles. James, Cephas [Peter] and John, those esteemed as pillars, gave me and Barnabas the right hand of fellowship when they recognized the grace given to me. They agreed that we should go to the Gentiles, and they to the circumcised. All they asked was that we should continue to remember the poor, the very thing I had been eager to do all along. (Galatians 2:1–10)

Scholars are uncertain as to the time and date of this meeting in Jerusalem. Some view it as Paul's account of the Jerusalem Council referenced by Luke in Acts 15. Others see this as a different meeting entirely. Sound arguments can be advanced for both positions. Regardless of the chronology of this meeting, it is obvious that Paul recognizes James, Peter, and John as *"esteemed pillars"* in the church. In addition, he sees himself as accountable to them for the integrity of the message he preaches to the Gentiles. By extension he considers their endorsement as lending credence to his message and his apostleship. Their acceptance of the uncircumcised Titus into fellowship buttresses his argument that adherence to the Mosaic Law was not required for Gentile believers.

Since James the brother of Jesus was not initially a leader within the church, how did he come to play such a significant role, as revealed in Acts 15? The Galatians passage above provides some evidence. Paul recognizes James, Cephas (Peter), and John as *"esteemed pillars."* When did James enter into this esteemed position? The first chapter of Acts provides some tantalizing clues.

After Christ's ascension Peter initiated a meeting of the remaining eleven apostles to find a replacement for Judas the traitor. Peter reasoned from scripture that they should appoint someone in order to return to the original configuration of twelve apostles.

> "For," said Peter, "it is written in the Book of Psalms:
> "'May his place be deserted; let there be no one to dwell in it,' and, "'May another take his place of leadership.'
> "Therefore it is necessary to choose one of the men who have been with us the whole time the Lord Jesus was living among us, beginning from John's baptism to the time when Jesus was taken up from us. For one of these must become a witness with us of his resurrection."
> So they nominated two men: Joseph called Barsabbas (also known as Justus) and Matthias. Then they prayed, "Lord, you know everyone's heart. Show us

which of these two you have chosen to take over this apostolic ministry, which Judas left to go where he belongs." Then they cast lots, and the lot fell to Matthias; so he was added to the eleven apostles. (Acts 1:20–26)

This raises an interesting question. If Peter, with the agreement of the remaining eleven, felt it necessary to appoint a new apostle to replace the deceased Judas, did he or John initiate the same response following the death of James the son of Zebedee in Acts chapter 12?

As pointed out in Chapter 2, during his ministry Jesus always had an inner circle of three. The canon provides no definitive answer to this question of apostolic succession, but it is from this point on that James begins to play a prominent role in the Acts account. Did James, the brother of Jesus, simply replace James the son of Zebedee, who was the brother of the Apostle John? If past practice is any indication, then this may well be the case. Furthermore, Paul's identification of James among the triumvirate of esteemed pillars in Galatians 2 lends credence to this view.

Despite a certain spiritual affinity between James and Paul, and the similarity in their conversion experiences, a tension exists between them. It is a tension that quite naturally arises from the constituency that they serve. James was the servant leader of the Jewish church; Paul saw himself as the servant leader of the Gentile church. Quite naturally there was a greater adherence to and appreciation of the Mosaic Law among Jewish believers in Christ. This was an integral part of their heritage. Their new-found faith in Jesus as Messiah did not mean they would give up all aspects of their Jewish faith. On the contrary, many may have gained a deeper appreciation for it. A misdirected zeal for the law would bring some of them into conflict with Gentile believers who had no such heritage.

From Paul's perspective we can see some of this conflict:

When Cephas [Peter] came to Antioch, I opposed him to his face, because he stood condemned. For before certain men came from James, he used to eat with the

Gentiles. But when they arrived, he began to draw back and separate himself from the Gentiles because he was afraid of those who belonged to the circumcision group. The other Jews joined him in his hypocrisy, so that by their hypocrisy even Barnabas was led astray.

When I saw that they were not acting in line with the truth of the gospel, I said to Cephas in front of them all, "You are a Jew, yet you live like a Gentile and not like a Jew. How is it, then, that you force Gentiles to follow Jewish customs?

"We who are Jews by birth and not sinful Gentiles know that a person is not justified by the works of the law, but by faith in Jesus Christ. So we, too, have put our faith in Christ Jesus that we may be justified by faith in Christ and not by the works of the law, because by the works of the law no one will be justified. (Galatians 2:11–16)

It is clear from this passage that a dichotomy of faith-based dietary practise separated Jewish and Gentile Christians and even seasoned veterans such as Peter and Barnabas had difficulty straddling this divide. How inclusive was Christian fellowship if Jewish and Gentile Christians could not dine together? Paul was justified in calling his apostolic colleagues to account. If all are justified by faith in Christ, then separation into distinct camps for mealtimes signalled a divided church.

One should not assume that the "*certain men*" who "*came from James*" were strict advocates of circumcision for Gentile believers. The text does not allow us to reach this conclusion. They simply may have decided to adhere to a set of dietary scruples that were the norm in a fully Jewish society. But by transferring these uncompromised scruples to a mixed setting of Jews and Gentiles, they fixed a gulf between the two parties. Whether that was their intend is not clear, but the division it signalled was unmistakable.

The bigger issue is the hypocrisy that was displayed by both Peter and Barnabas. Previously they had eaten with the Gentiles. Were they worried that these men from James would tattle on them? Would James disapprove of them eating with Gentiles? Judging by his conciliatory stance at the Jerusalem Council it is doubtful that James would disapprove. In fact, much of his judgment in Acts 15 is aimed at making cross-cultural fellowship at mealtime possible.

In his commentary on this passage from Galatians, R.A. Cole makes this pertinent observation: "We give much thought to the problems of Paul, but few to those of James. This is scarcely equitable, especially in view of the vast range of opinion among Jewish Christendom."[104]

As the leader of the Jerusalem church, James was tasked with maintaining unity in Jewish Christendom—a near impossible task. If, as legend has it, James spent much of his time on his knees in prayer, here would be the reason for his earnest petition. He had within his ranks many from the party of the Pharisees.[105] Though they believed in Christ's atoning sacrifice, in all likelihood they also considered adherence to Mosaic Law as sacrosanct. Balancing this off with those of more liberated views was next to impossible. This became even more difficult when trying to find a degree of accommodation with an influx of Gentile believers.

It's quite easy to understand why Paul and his Gentile followers would resist embracing circumcision and the stringent minutia of Mosaic Law. But when we reverse the position, is it logical to assume that because of their new-found liberty in Christ, Jewish believers should no longer circumcise their sons and begin eating pork? Modern Jewish converts to Christianity face the same dilemma. In their embrace of Christ, must they jettison all elements of their Jewish faith, or should they maintain some or all aspects of it? Through the ages the response to these questions has been varied. Undoubtedly, James attempted to maintain a spirit of Christian unity among those who responded differently to these questions.

R. A. Cole sees these "*certain men*" who "*came from James*" as representative of the more conservative or legalistic Jewish believers: "They

---

[104] R. A. Cole, *The Epistle of Paul to the Galatians—Tyndale New Testament Commentaries* (Eerdmans, 1984), p. 75.

[105] Acts 15:5.

were clearly his [James'] own 'right wing', the Pharisaic group, and a sore embarrassment even to him."[106]

For James to balance these divergent views and maintain Christian unity was a herculean task. In a world of ethnic, racial and religious divisions, Christian unity—unity in the Spirit—is a miracle no less significant than the feeding of the five thousand or the healing of the paralytic.

There are theologians who emphasize the differences between Paul and James. Paul emphasized grace and faith, while in his epistle the practical-minded James emphasized doing the commands of Christ. But like James, Paul ends many of his epistles with a to-do list for practical Christian living.[107] And like Paul, James speaks of a spiritual rebirth through the word—a doctrine that is universal among New Testament authors.[108] In short, there is far more that unites these founding pillars of the faith than divides them. They are engaged in building something totally new—a grand cross-cultural experiment called the church.

Paul called this fusion of Gentiles and Jews into the church a mystery.

In reading this, then, you will be able to understand my insight into the mystery of Christ, which was not made known to people in other generations as it has now been revealed by the Spirit to God's holy apostles and prophets. This mystery is that through the gospel the Gentiles are heirs together with Israel, members together of one body, and sharers together in the promise in Christ Jesus. (Ephesians 3:4–6)

Building and maintaining unity in Christ across a huge cultural and religious divide was an integral part of Paul's mission. It should be remembered that in almost all cases Paul began his church planting mission to a community by preaching at the local Jewish synagogue. He continued there until the Jewish community rejected his message. Only

---

[106] Cole, *Galatians*, p. 75.

[107] Galatians 6:1–10, Ephesians 5:1–6:9, Philippians 4:4-9, Colossians 3:1–4:6, 1 Thessalonians 4:1–5:22.

[108] James 1:18.

then did he go directly to the Gentiles—but he always drew some Jewish converts to Christ with him.[109] The congregations that formed were a blend of Jewish and Gentile believers.

We need to keep in mind that James endorsed Paul's ministry. According to Luke there was joy among the Jewish believers when they heard the news of Gentiles turning to the Lord.[110] James surely joined in this rejoicing. In addition, at the Jerusalem Council he opened wide the door to the Gentile believers entering the church by placing very few restrictions on them. He did not require them to be circumcised.

According to Jewish tradition, there are 613 commandments (*mitzvot*) in the Law of Moses, covering virtually every aspect of daily life. But in a single bold stroke, the Jerusalem Council at James' direction set aside all of these but three. To take such a position, James must have been in full agreement with Paul's assertion in Galatians 2:15-16.

> We who are Jews by birth and not sinful Gentiles know that a person is not justified by the works of the law, but by faith in Jesus Christ. So we, too, have put our faith in Christ Jesus that we may be justified by faith in Christ and not by the works of the law, because by the works of the law no one will be justified. (Galatians 2:15–16)

Spiritual rebirth through faith in Christ was the crucial factor that made one a Christian, not circumcision or adherence to the Mosaic Law. James fully grasped this because he personally experienced it. Just like Paul, though he was circumcised and strictly observant of the Law, James initially did not believe in Christ. Saving faith was born in him on the day he encountered his resurrected brother.

Rather than being at loggerheads as some theologians would have us believe, Paul and James were full partners in the spread of the gospel. Rather than be appalled at the news that Gentile and Jewish Christians

---

[109] For an example of Paul's methodology in evangelizing a community, read Acts 13:13–52.

[110] See Acts 11:18, Acts 15:3–4, and Acts 21:19–20.

were eating together in Galatia, James would have rejoiced in their show of unity. After all, at the Jerusalem Council he established a set of rules to make such fellowship possible.

In Paul's letter to the Galatians, we see that James had within his ranks Jewish Christ followers who saw these matters differently. Some of them stirred up a great deal of trouble among the Gentile believers. But rather than see James and Paul as theological opponents, we should view them as bridge builders who worked together to advance the gospel within their assigned field and across cultural and racial barriers. Today, in the context of a rising tide of Christian nationalism, there is an urgent need for ministers of the gospel to do the same.

Why did James come to play such a pivotal role in the early church? Perhaps the best answer may be because he was a conciliator and a bridge builder at a time when the church was rapidly expanding into new territory and across people groups. In other words, he was the right man at the right time for the job.

But in the final analysis, something more fundamental may have been the deciding factor in James' rise to prominence. That factor is the Jewish understanding of inheritance. According to the Law of Moses, the bride of a deceased brother who has no male heir must be given to the next brother in line, so that he can father a child to continue his brother's lineage.

> If brothers are living together and one of them dies without a son, his widow must not marry outside the family. Her husband's brother shall take her and marry her and fulfill the duty of a brother-in-law to her. The first son she bears shall carry on the name of the dead brother so that his name will not be blotted out from Israel. (Deuteronomy 25:5–6)

Jesus' departure from the earth meant that all his earthly possessions would legally pass to his next surviving brother. In this case, that would be James. Jesus had no substantial material inheritance. And he had no wife—or did he?

Throughout the New Testament the church is referred to as the bride of Christ.[111] If the church is Christ's bride, then it logically follows that in his physical absence the responsibility for the care of the bride should fall to Christ's brother.

As long as James was outside the household of faith as established by Jesus, he had no right to this inherited responsibility. But having been born again by the Spirit, James now had a dual claim to Christ's bride, the church, by virtue of both natural and spiritual DNA. Furthermore, over time he had proven himself as a loyal follower and a developing leader within the church, as shown in the Book of Acts.

The early apostles were all well-versed in Jewish laws of succession. They may well have viewed James' ascent to leadership as the right and lawful outcome. It prevented the leadership squabbling and jockeying for position evident while Christ was still present with them. It handily settled the question of leadership posed by the mother of James and John, the sons of Zebedee.

> Then the mother of Zebedee's sons came to Jesus with her sons and, kneeling down, asked a favor of him.
>
> "What is it you want?" he asked.
>
> She said, "Grant that one of these two sons of mine may sit at your right and the other at your left in your kingdom."
>
> "You don't know what you are asking," Jesus said to them. "Can you drink the cup I am going to drink?"
>
> "We can," they answered.
>
> Jesus said to them, "You will indeed drink from my cup, but to sit at my right or left is not for me to grant. These places belong to those for whom they have been prepared by my Father."
>
> When the ten heard about this, they were indignant with the two brothers. Jesus called them together and said, "You know that the rulers of the Gentiles lord

[111] See Ephesians 5:22–33, 2 Corinthians 11:2, Revelations 19:7, Revelations 21:2, Revelations 21:9, Revelations 22:17.

158

it over them, and their high officials exercise authority over them. Not so with you. Instead, whoever wants to become great among you must be your servant, and whoever wants to be first must be your slave—just as the Son of Man did not come to be served, but to serve, and to give his life as a ransom for many." (Matthew 20:20–28)

Which of the twelve would lead? Peter, James, or John? Jesus side-stepped the question. His Father would decide. And in the end Jesus' Father bypassed all three. He settled on James, the son of Joseph, the brother of Jesus.[112]

---

[112] Jesus validated the Jewish practice of fraternal succession in marriage in his discourse with the Sadducees. See Matthew 22:23–33.

$$---15---$$

James Reconciling the Irreconcilable

I n the scriptural record our next encounter with James is in the twen-
ty-first chapter of Acts. It occurs due to a commitment (cited previously) that the apostle Paul made to James, Peter, and John, regarding
help for the poor in Jerusalem:

> James, Cephas [Peter] and John, those esteemed as pil-
> lars, gave me and Barnabas the right hand of fellow-
> ship when they recognized the grace given to me. They
> agreed that we should go to the Gentiles, and they to
> the circumcised. All they asked was that we should
> continue to remember the poor, the very thing I had
> been eager to do all along. (Galatians 2:9–10)

Apparently, Paul took this commitment seriously. A considerable
portion of his ministry involved raising financial support for the poor in
the Jerusalem church. He devotes two chapters of his second letter to the
Corinthians solely to the topic of collecting an offering for this purpose.
He also sent Titus his trusted lieutenant and other brothers ahead to be
sure that the church's offering was ready to be received upon his arrival
(2 Corinthians 8:16–9:5). It is evident from these two chapters that

this endeavor entailed a great deal of effort and strategic planning. Nor was this an isolated event involving only one church. As Paul travelled through his circuit of church plants, he took up an offering for the destitute believers in Jerusalem in each city. Paul justified his actions with these words:

> This service that you perform is not only supplying the needs of the Lord's people but is also overflowing in many expressions of thanks to God. Because of the service by which you have proved yourselves, others will praise God for the obedience that accompanies your confession of the gospel of Christ, and for your generosity in sharing with them and with everyone else. And in their prayers for you their hearts will go out to you, because of the surpassing grace God has given you. Thanks be to God for his indescribable gift! (2 Corinthians 9:12–15)

It is clear from this statement that Paul saw this offering as a way to build bridges between the Gentile and Jewish Christian communities. Presumably this is part of the reason why James, Peter, and John originally proposed it—that and a genuine concern for the poor. Care for the poor is a prominent teaching in the Epistle of James.[113]

Poverty seems to have been common among the Christian believers in Jerusalem and a top-of-mind concern for James. There could be several reasons for this poverty. The early church appears to have attracted a large number of poor. Perhaps this was because Jesus' personal ministry drew attention to the marginalized, to social outcasts, tax collectors, and sinners.[114] Early on the church in Jerusalem established a charitable ministry to help widows and orphans, and this likely attracted others who were also in need.[115]

---

[113] James 1:9, 2:1–7, 2:15–16.

[114] See Luke 15:1–2, Matthew 9:10–11, Mark 2:15–16, Matthew 21:31–32.

[115] See Acts 6:1–7.

Persecution also ravished the church. From accounts in Acts we know this included death and imprisonment,[116] but it likely also involved a loss of employment or advancement and possibly the destruction or seizure of property. Paul in his earlier life as Saul, the persecutor of the church, had contributed to this impoverishment. This surely was a motivating factor for Paul as he tried to make amends for his former conduct.

Finally, the communal lifestyle that the community adopted likely contributed to the general state of poverty.

> All the believers were together and had everything in common. They sold property and possessions to give to anyone who had need. Every day they continued to meet together in the temple courts. They broke bread in their homes and ate together with glad and sincere hearts, praising God and enjoying the favor of all the people. And the Lord added to their number daily those who were being saved. (Acts 2:44–47)

As long as the Christian community was growing, this communal system of care would work well, since there would be a constant supply of fresh funds coming from new converts. But if growth stagnated the result would be mutual poverty. If lands and houses were sold and the capital was used on consumables like food and clothing, long-term sustainability would be in jeopardy.

> All the believers were one in heart and mind. No one claimed that any of their possessions was their own, but they shared everything they had. With great power the apostles continued to testify to the resurrection of the Lord Jesus. And God's grace was so powerfully at work in them all that there were no needy persons among them. For from time to time those who owned land or houses sold them, brought the money from the

---

[116] See Acts 8:3 and 22:4.

sales and put it at the apostles' feet, and it was distrib-
uted to anyone who had need. (Acts 4:32–35)

At some point the scenario of general well-being and prosperity described above may have turned to widespread poverty. It seems likely
that funds from the burgeoning Gentile church were needed to sustain
this early experiment in communal living, hence the request recorded in
Galatians that Paul should *remember the poor.*"

This is the situation that James, as leader of the Jerusalem church,
finds himself in Acts 21. He oversees an established church that appears
to have plateaued. Growth has slowed, but the needs of the poor remain
constant.

But even before Paul arrives in Jerusalem, he is forewarned that
things will not go well for him there.

> After we had been there a number of days, a prophet
> named Agabus came down from Judea. Coming over
> to us, he took Paul's belt, tied his own hands and feet
> with it and said, "The Holy Spirit says, 'In this way the
> Jewish leaders in Jerusalem will bind the owner of this
> belt and will hand him over to the Gentiles.'" (Acts
> 21:10–11)

But despite this warning, Paul would not turn back, saying he was
"willing to die in Jerusalem for the name of the Lord Jesus" (Acts 21:12–14).

Luke's description of the arrival of Paul's delegation in Jerusalem
gives us considerable insight into James' position in the church and the
state of relations between these two men.

> When we arrived at Jerusalem, the brothers and sisters
> received us warmly. The next day Paul and the rest of
> us went to see James, and all the elders were present.
> Paul greeted them and reported in detail what God had
> done among the Gentiles through his ministry. (Acts
> 21:17–19)

Did the elders who were present include some of Christ's original twelve apostles? The text is not clear on this point, since the only apostle named in this circle of leaders is James.

Howard Marshall, in his commentary on this passage, observes that James "by this point had fully assumed the leadership of the church in Jerusalem."[117]

We are told Paul specifically went to see James.

Firstly, this would indicate that there was an ongoing friendly relationship between James and Paul. This is reinforced by Paul's statements cited earlier in his letter to the Galatians and by his earlier report to the Council of Jerusalem in the fifteenth chapter of Acts.

Secondly, it implies that Paul considers himself accountable to James. We are told he *"reported in detail what God had done among the Gentiles through his ministry."*

One is left with the impression that Paul sees himself as a humble servant of Christ and the church. He has returned to Jerusalem, the home base and headquarters of the church,[118] to present a generous offering for the support of the needy among the believers there.

Moreover, he sees himself as accountable for his actions and ministry to James the head of the church, so he delivers his detailed report before him. In many ways this resembles the procedures of churches or agencies that send missionaries today. The missionary from time to time is expected to report on the successes and challenges of his mission.

Paul's first mission report was delivered to his sending church, the church in Antioch.[119] Later, in about 50 AD, he presents a report of pivotal importance to the Council of Jerusalem.[120] This then is his third report and his second one before James in Jerusalem.

It should be noted that Paul was accompanied by uncircumcised Gentile converts, Luke the author of Acts being one of them.

---

[117] Marshall, *The Acts of the Apostles*, p. 342.

[118] See Acts 1:8.

[119] See Acts 14:27–28.

[120] See Acts 15:12.

Paul's report draws a rather lengthy response that gives us considerable insight into the mind of James and the state of the church in Jerusalem.

> When they heard this, they praised God. Then they said to Paul: "You see, brother, how many thousands of Jews have believed, and all of them are zealous for the law. They have been informed that you teach all the Jews who live among the Gentiles to turn away from Moses, telling them not to circumcise their children or live according to our customs. What shall we do? They will certainly hear that you have come, so do what we tell you. There are four men with us who have made a vow. Take these men, join in their purification rites and pay their expenses, so that they can have their heads shaved. Then everyone will know there is no truth in these reports about you, but that you yourself are living in obedience to the law. As for the Gentile believers, we have written to them our decision that they should abstain from food sacrificed to idols, from blood, from the meat of strangled animals and from sexual immorality." (Acts 21: 20–25)

Who spoke the words shown within the quotation marks? Luke, the author, attributes these words to *"they"*—they being *"James, and all the elders."* It is implausible that James and the elders spoke these words in unison. Most likely the statement Luke recorded is an accurate summation of their discussion—a discussion over which James presides. It logically follows that this statement provides a glimpse into the mind of James and the elders around him.

First, we are told *"they praised God"* on hearing Paul's report of his ministry among the Gentiles. This signals James' approval of Paul's ministry and his specific call to reach the Gentiles.

As previously noted, Paul was not alone when he presented his report to James and the elders. He was accompanied by a number of

Gentile believers. Luke uses the phrase "*Paul and the rest of us*" (Acts 21:18), thereby indicating his inclusion in Paul's delegation during the day's proceedings.

The presence of these Gentile followers of Christ certainly would have added weight to Paul's report. These men were living proof of the grace of God being poured out on the Gentiles.

It makes sense that James would draw a good deal of satisfaction from Paul's report, since it vindicated his previous ruling at the Jerusalem Council to open the door of faith to the Gentiles.

Paul's report provided ample evidence that God endorsed this radical shift in policy. First, his ministry was accompanied by heaven-sent signs and wonders. Secondly, in quick succession he was establishing local churches in Asia Minor, Macedonia, and Greece. Thirdly, these churches were thriving to the point where they were providing financial support for the church in Jerusalem.

But Paul's success brought with it a dilemma. In the response to Paul's report we are told that in Jerusalem "*many thousands of Jews have believed, and all of them are zealous for the law.*" This zeal for the law presented a problem, since it had the potential of creating a deep cultural rift within the church. To ameliorate this problem, James and the leaders around him propose a bridge building exercise between Paul and these Jewish Christians.

Most often when divisions arise within an organization, misinformation lies at the root. That certainly was the case here. According to the above statement, the believers in Jerusalem "*have been informed that you teach all the Jews who live among the Gentiles to turn away from Moses, telling them not to circumcise their children or live according to our customs.*"

None of this is true and James knows this, but to set the record straight and prove Paul's adherence to the law, he is advised to take part in a purification rite with four other men.

Despite Paul's insistence that Gentile believers need not be circumcised (Galatians 5:2–6), he did not give such advice to Jewish followers of Christ. In fact, he did just the opposite. Timothy, Paul's personal disciple, is a case in point. Timothy's mother was Jewish, but his father was Greek. Before setting out on one of his journeys, Paul circumcised him.

Paul wanted to take him [Timothy] along on the journey, so he circumcised him because of the Jews who lived in that area, for they all knew that his father was a Greek. As they traveled from town to town, they delivered the decisions reached by the apostles and elders in Jerusalem for the people to obey. So the churches were strengthened in the faith and grew daily in numbers. (Acts 16:3–5)

What is most remarkable about this example of circumcision is that Paul did this while going about delivering the Jerusalem Council's ruling that Gentiles need not be circumcised. The reason given for doing this circumcision reveals a great deal about Paul's methodology. We are told that this was done *because of the Jews who lived in that area, for they all knew that his father was a Greek.*

Why would the opinion of the Jews in the area matter to Paul? Wasn't he free from the rule of the law and living under the grace of Christ? By extension, why would Paul submit to participate in purification rites as prescribed by James and the elders in Jerusalem? We can find the answer in Paul's second letter to the Corinthians.

Though I am free and belong to no one, I have made myself a slave to everyone, to win as many as possible. To the Jews I became like a Jew, to win the Jews. To those under the law I became like one under the law (though I myself am not under the law), so as to win those under the law. To those not having the law I became like one not having the law (though I am not free from God's law but am under Christ's law), so as to win those not having the law. To the weak I became weak, to win the weak. I have become all things to all people so that by all possible means I might save some. I do all this for the sake of the gospel, that I may share in its blessings. (2 Corinthians 9:19–23)

Paul's purpose was evangelism. He wanted to "*save some*." He wanted to win the Jews in the vicinity of Timothy's hometown over to faith in Christ. The same motivation would have been at work as Paul returned to Jerusalem. He wanted the gospel presented in the best light possible. If submitting to religious observances helped prepare people's hearts to hear the gospel message, Paul was willing to oblige.

But this desire that motivated Paul also motivated James. James wanted the entire Jewish nation won over to the gospel. He wanted his people to embrace the message of redemption through the death, burial, and resurrection of Jesus Christ. This is after all the express mission of the church.

There are theologians who see vastly different motives at work in James and Paul, but a careful reading of the scriptures does not bear this out. There is no indication that Paul chafed at this recommendation to undergo ritual purification. He submitted to it willingly because he wanted to correct the erroneous perception that he had abandoned the law and was encouraging other Jewish converts to do the same.

It should be noted that this erroneous perception existed among Christian Jews who were "*zealous for the law*." As we shall see, the perception of unbelieving Jews was that Paul was worthy of death. The first bridge that needed to be built or repaired was between Paul and Jewish believers. Paul would go to great lengths for the sake of cross-cultural Christian unity.

All of this was part of Paul's grand vision for the church. His great desire was to have Jews and Gentiles united as one under Christ. He gives voice to this thought in his Epistle to the Ephesians.

> Therefore, remember that formerly you who are Gentiles by birth and called "uncircumcised" by those who call themselves "the circumcision" (which is done in the body by human hands)—remember that at that time you were separate from Christ, excluded from citizenship in Israel and foreigners to the covenants of the promise, without hope and without God in the world.

> But now in Christ Jesus you who once were far away
> have been brought near by the blood of Christ.
>
> For he himself is our peace, who has made the two
> groups one and has destroyed the barrier, the dividing
> wall of hostility, by setting aside in his flesh the law
> with its commands and regulations. His purpose was
> to create in himself one new humanity out of the two,
> thus making peace, and in one body to reconcile both
> of them to God through the cross, by which he put to
> death their hostility. (Ephesians 2:11–16)

In very practical, tangible terms, Paul is trying to make peace and work at reconciliation between Jews and Gentiles. Paul does this by participating in the prescribed purification rites at the urging of James. These are precisely the laws, commands, and regulations which Christ set aside, according to the statement above.

Typically, these events are viewed from Paul's perspective, but it is James who sits at the center these two camps—or is it four camps? James is trying to reconcile Paul and his Gentile converts with the Christ-following, law-abiding Jews within his flock. James has a measure of sway over these two camps, due to his leadership role and the Spirit of Christ within him.

But beyond these two camps lies the broader Jewish and Gentile world. Both realms are innately hostile to the gospel. Yet as James sees it and Jesus' Great Commission declares[121] the church is charged with reaching both these worlds.

James is fully vested in seeing both worlds reconciled to his brother, the Lord Jesus Christ. That's why he endorsed Paul's ministry at the Council of Jerusalem. That's why he set the bar very low for Gentile entry into the church. And that's why he rejoiced over Paul's missionary report of rapid church growth among the Gentiles.

The Gentiles were being reconciled to Christ.

Full reconciliation cost Jesus his life. In this situation attempted reconciliation almost cost Paul his life. When hearts become hard, it takes a

---

[121] Matthew 28:18–20, Mark 16:15–20.

miracle to reconcile the irreconcilable. In this instance no miracle came. Whereas many hearts in the Gentile world were opening to Christ, in the Jewish world we see hearts are hardening.

> When the seven days were nearly over, some Jews from the province of Asia saw Paul at the temple. They stirred up the whole crowd and seized him, shouting, "Fellow Israelites, help us! This is the man who teaches everyone everywhere against our people and our law and this place. And besides, he has brought Greeks into the temple and defiled this holy place." (They had previously seen Trophimus the Ephesian in the city with Paul and assumed that Paul had brought him into the temple.)
>
> The whole city was aroused, and the people came running from all directions. Seizing Paul, they dragged him from the temple, and immediately the gates were shut. While they were trying to kill him, news reached the commander of the Roman troops that the whole city of Jerusalem was in an uproar. He at once took some officers and soldiers and ran down to the crowd. When the rioters saw the commander and his soldiers, they stopped beating Paul. The commander came up and arrested him and ordered him to be bound with two chains. (Acts 21:27–33a)

There can be no doubt that the intervention of this Gentile commanding officer saved Paul from certain death at the hands of his countrymen.

It was James who sent Paul on this dangerous and futile attempt at cross-cultural bridge building, but there isn't the slightest hint of anger or regret on Paul's part during the events that follow. He does not blame James for his subsequent arrest and imprisonment. He sees it as part of the will and purpose of God for his life. He embraces his suffering and makes the most of his opportunities to be a witness for Christ before the

Jewish mob, Roman authorities, the Sanhedrin, Governors Felix and Festus, and King Agrippa and Bernice.[122] Ultimately his defence of the gospel will bring him before the emperor in Rome.

Paul sees all this as the fulfilment of his divine mandate received from Christ. Rather than viewing his imprisonment as a hindrance, he sees it as an opportunity.

In light of Paul's arrest and imprisonment, did James have any regrets for counseling Paul to engage in this ritual purification? There is no indication of that. The apostles wore persecution and suffering for Christ as a badge of honor.[123]

James' advice to Paul while in prison would likely be in line with the opening words of his epistle.

> Consider it pure joy, my brothers and sisters, whenever you face trials of many kinds, because you know that the testing of your faith produces perseverance. Let perseverance finish its work so that you may be mature and complete, not lacking anything. (James 1:2–4)

In these matters, James was simply following his brother's counsel as expressed in the concluding words of the Beatitudes.

> Blessed are those who are persecuted because of righteousness, for theirs is the kingdom of heaven.
>
> Blessed are you when people insult you, persecute you and falsely say all kinds of evil against you because of me. Rejoice and be glad, because great is your reward in heaven, for in the same way they persecuted the prophets who were before you. (Matthew 5:10–12)

The interaction between James and Paul in Acts 21 is the last occasion when we meet James within the pages of the Book of Acts. We see an apostle and a leader in his prime. He is exercising his authority

---

[122] See Acts 21:37–26:32.

[123] See Acts 5:40–42 and 2 Corinthians 11:16–29.

over the church—an authority that extends beyond the local church in Jerusalem. The apostle Paul—the leading thinker, evangelist, and author of half the New Testament—reports to James and is accountable to him.

This raises the question: Were the other apostles accountable to James as well?

It could be argued that Paul may have developed a special relationship or bond with James. It may be that Paul saw himself as a disciple of James, and this is why Paul submits to him for counsel and advice.

But at the Council of Jerusalem in Acts 15, both Peter and Paul give reports in a meeting over which James presides. Though not explicitly stated, Luke's account of the church meetings of Acts 15 and Acts 21 leave the distinct impression that James was functioning as the head of the church.

When we encounter James in Paul's epistles, we are left with a similar impression. Paul sees Peter as a colleague, but he shows a deference and respect for James that one would expect toward someone in authority.[124]

In turn, Peter shows the same collegial respect toward Paul.[125]

The accounts in Acts and Galatians portray James as the overall leader of the church, but this contrasts sharply with the Roman Catholic position that Peter was the designated head of the church. In fact, there is little evidence to support the Catholic position within the Acts account or any of the epistles.

All of this has huge implications for church governance, and it goes to the root of many divisions we see across the church world today.

James lies at the heart of all these issues. But for many, James, the brother of Jesus, remains a great mystery—as enigmatic as the stone box that bears his name.

---

[124] See 1 Corinthians 15:7, Galatians 1:18–2:16.

[125] See 2 Peter 3:15–16.

—— 16 ——

James the Apostle to the Jews

Before we transition to an examination of the Epistle of James, it would be appropriate to examine the Jewish roots of the church. No one in the early church embodies the Jewishness of this entity we call the church quite like James. And no event in the history of the early church illustrates Christianity's link to Judaism quite like James' decision in Acts 21 that Paul should participate in ritual cleansing at the temple.

Today Christians and Jews see their religions as distinct from each other. The decisions and actions of both James and Paul show that they did not share this view.

James was leading a profoundly Jewish church. He says as much. *"You see, brother [Paul], how many thousands of Jews have believed, and all of them are zealous for the law"* (Acts 21:20).

These believing Jews were not only zealous for law. They were also zealous for the temple and had not in any way abandoned the practices and ceremonies of temple worship. As James and the elders point out, four of their company—believers in Christ—were fulfilling vows and participating in purification rites. It should be noted that from Pentecost onward, believers were meeting daily in the Temple (Acts 2:46–47), and there are strong indications that this practice continued.

To Christians today, this may seem incomprehensible. We have well-established dividing lines that separate Jews from Christians and Judaism from Christianity. For James no such line existed.

A modern equivalent might be a televangelist having his infant daughter baptized at a cathedral by a Catholic archbishop. Or conversely, the televangelist might do a full immersion baptism of the archbishop. Yet both these examples fall under the broad tent of the Christian faith. But both James and Paul were even more radical. They were comfortable stepping across lines that we have established between two great faiths, Christianity and Judaism.

Some of our difficulties spring from a lack of understanding of this fusion of faith within the early Jewish Christian community. They saw Jesus as their Jewish Messiah, fulfilling all the prophecies of their scriptures. He did not come to do away with their faith or the Law, but to fulfill it—and he said just that.

> Do not think that I have come to abolish the Law or the Prophets; I have not come to abolish them but to fulfill them. For truly I tell you, until heaven and earth disappear, not the smallest letter, not the least stroke of a pen, will by any means disappear from the Law until everything is accomplished. Therefore anyone who sets aside one of the least of these commands and teaches others accordingly will be called least in the kingdom of heaven, but whoever practices and teaches these commands will be called great in the kingdom of heaven. For I tell you that unless your righteousness surpasses that of the Pharisees and the teachers of the law, you will certainly not enter the kingdom of heaven. (Matthew 5:17–20)

Also, Jesus in no way encouraged disobedience to the Law. Many Christians have a false impression of Jesus and his teaching. They assume that because he was supremely loving and forgiving, he must have been lax in his application of the Law or easy-going about sin. Just the opposite is true, and his statements recorded in the gospels make this abundantly clear.

Rather than lower the bar in his Sermon on the Mount, Jesus elevates it. The Old Testament law prohibits murder; Jesus prohibits hate (Matthew 5:21–22). The Old Testament law prohibits adultery; Jesus prohibits lust (Matthew 5:27–28). He systematically demands more than the law requires by going to the heart of the issue, rather than simply looking at outward appearance or performance.

While Jesus condemned the hypocrisy and pride of the Pharisees and teachers of the law, he did not quibble with their adherence to it.

> Woe to you, teachers of the law and Pharisees, you hypocrites! You give a tenth of your spices—mint, dill and cumin. But you have neglected the more important matters of the law—justice, mercy and faithfulness. You should have practiced the latter, without neglecting the former. You blind guides! You strain out a gnat but swallow a camel (Matthew 23:23–24)

Similarly, Jesus did not abandon temple worship. If anything, he was an advocate for it. His cleansing of the temple was not an indictment of temple worship, but an attack on the abuse of that sacred space. He viewed the temple grounds as the rightful place for prayer, praise, healing, and the teaching of the word.

> Jesus entered the temple courts and drove out all who were buying and selling there. He overturned the tables of the money changers and the benches of those selling doves. "It is written," he said to them, "'My house will be called a house of prayer,' but you are making it 'a den of robbers.'"
>
> The blind and the lame came to him at the temple, and he healed them. But when the chief priests and the teachers of the law saw the wonderful things he did and

the children shouting in the temple courts, "Hosanna to the Son of David," they were indignant.

"Do you hear what these children are saying?" they asked him.

"Yes," replied Jesus, "have you never read, 'From the lips of children and infants you, Lord, have called forth your praise?'" (Matthew 21:12–16)

In the same vein, though Jesus prophesied the destruction of the temple (Matthew 24:1–2), that prophecy should not be viewed as a vindictive declaration, but rather a lament.

> As he approached Jerusalem and saw the city, he wept over it and said, "If you, even you, had only known on this day what would bring you peace—but now it is hidden from your eyes. The days will come upon you when your enemies will build an embankment against you and encircle you and hem you in on every side. They will dash you to the ground, you and the children within your walls. They will not leave one stone on another, because you did not recognize the time of God's coming to you." (Luke 19:41–44)

The conflict that led to Jesus' crucifixion can be viewed as a dispute over the proper use of the temple. The high priest and temple authorities were enraged over the eviction of the merchants and money changers because they benefitted from this trade—and it was of course a direct challenge to their authority. In his commentary on this matter, William Barclay makes this assessment on the trade in sacrificial doves:

> Clearly he [Jesus] had attacked this abuse. Further, these stalls where the victims were sold were called the Bazaars of Annas, and were the private property of the family of the high priest of that name.[126]

---

[126] William Barclay, *The Gospel of Matthew, Volume Two, Chapters 11–28—The Daily Study Bible* (Welch, 1975), p. 246.

In addition, the high priest and his clan objected to Jesus' use of the temple as his teaching and healing center.

For Jesus this issue went to the heart of his DNA. It was about being at home in his Father's house and using it according to His will and purpose. It harkens back to his first recorded words as a twelve-year-old boy, "*Didn't you know I had to be in my Father's house?*" (Luke 2:49)

Furthermore, it was about the fulfilment of his prophetic mandate within this sacred precinct.

> "I will send my messenger, who will prepare the way before me. Then suddenly the Lord you are seeking will come to his temple; the messenger of the covenant, whom you desire, will come," says the LORD Almighty. (Malachi 3:1)

The Messiah had come to his temple, but the Jewish leadership was not prepared for him and refused to recognize him as their Lord.

There are strong indications that the apostles, including James, were fully at one with Jesus' view of the temple and its proper use and purpose. They saw it as their prayer and worship center and the rightful home of their Messiah.

The apostles did not relinquish the dispute that Jesus had initiated. They were not advocating for the temple's destruction, though they were accused of this (Acts 6:13-14). Rather, their goal was to turn the entire Jewish nation into believers in Jesus Christ, with the temple being used as their prayer and worship center.

The first physical healing recorded in Acts lends credence to this view.[127] Peter and John went to the temple at the appointed time for prayer. At the Beautiful Gate, they healed a man who was lame from birth through the power of Jesus' name. When in amazement a crowd gathered, they preached the gospel message.

Peter and John were doing precisely what Jesus had done in the temple courts before his arrest and crucifixion. They came to pray, they healed the infirm, and they taught the people about Christ. They also

---

[127] Acts 3:1–26.

got the same response from the authorities. They were arrested just as Jesus had been.

The story of this first miraculous healing of the apostolic age illustrates that rather than separate themselves, Peter and John participated in the rituals and practices of temple worship. They went to the temple at the hour of prayer—the time of the daily sacrifice—the time when Jesus, the pascal lamb, had offered up his life.

Because of persecution and fear, the Jewish church could have withdrawn entirely from the predominant culture—but it did just the opposite. The church inserted itself directly into the fabric of the community by meeting within the temple courts. "*The apostles performed many signs and wonders among the people. And all the believers used to meet together in Solomon's Colonnade.*" (Acts 5:12)

Solomon's Colonnade or Portico was part of the outer court of the temple.[128] Meeting there was an outright challenge to the Jewish religious authorities, and it also served as a bold witness to the believers' faith in the crucified and risen Christ—the Christ that these same authorities had sent to the cross. Despite arrests and warnings, they filled Jerusalem with their teaching (Acts 5:28).

It is well worth noting that the first public meeting place for the first century church was at the temple. This full, practical integration of Christianity with Judaism seems unnatural or contrary to us at the present. But James and the early believers didn't want to separate themselves from the Jewish people—they wanted to win over their hearts. In fact, they believed faith in Christ would make them better Jews, since they would be accepting the Messiah sent by the God of Israel.

James was situated at the center of an epic battle for the allegiance of his people. To understand him, we must understand how he viewed his apostolic mission and how he went about pursuing it.

As much as Paul identifies himself as the apostle to the Gentiles, James stands out as the apostle to the Jews. In Paul's letter to the Galatians, Paul self-identifies in this way, but he identifies Peter as the apostle to the Jews.

---

[128] "Solomon's Portico," by W. F. Stinespring, *The Interpreter's Dictionary of the Bible, Volume 4*, Edited by George Arthur Buttrick (Abingdon, 1984), p. 408.

> For God, who was at work in Peter as an apostle to the
> circumcised, was also at work in me as an apostle to
> the Gentiles. James, Cephas [Peter] and John, those es-
> teemed as pillars, gave me and Barnabas the right hand
> of fellowship when they recognized the grace given to
> me. They agreed that we should go to the Gentiles, and
> they to the circumcised. (Galatians 2:8–9)

As time progressed, Peter and John moved on to other fields—fields
that included the Gentiles—while James remained rooted in Jerusalem.
When we meet James in Acts 21, which may be as much as six years after
Paul's Galatian letter, it is apparent that James has assumed the mantle
of the apostle to the Jews.

Perhaps the greatest temptation James faced was the temptation to
withdraw from the culture and any involvement with the temple. To do
so would be to admit defeat. It would mean ceding the temple to those
who sanctioned his brother's execution. But James steadfastly refused to
turn his back on the Father's house.

The temptation for the church to withdraw from the culture rather
than engage with it remains to this day. Self-isolation is safer than being
an active and engaged witness to the life-transforming power of Christ.

James' instructions for Paul to participate in ceremonial cleansing
should be viewed as part of a broader strategy to be a potent witness for
Christ to the Jewish people. It was a strategy with which Paul agreed
because of his desire to see the salvation of his own people.

> Brothers and sisters, my heart's desire and prayer to
> God for the Israelites is that they may be saved. For I
> can testify about them that they are zealous for God,
> but their zeal is not based on knowledge. Since they
> did not know the righteousness of God and sought to
> establish their own, they did not submit to God's righ-
> teousness. Christ is the culmination of the law so that
> there may be righteousness for everyone who believes.
> (Romans 10:1–4)

Paul views the Jewish fixation on righteousness achieved by the law as a huge impediment to receiving the righteousness of Christ, which comes through faith. James, Paul, and Jesus agree on this point. Salvation for the Jewish people from Abraham onward was always achieved through faith—an active faith—not merely an intellectual acknowledgement.

It would be folly to assume that James and Paul did not discuss these foundational matters of faith on occasions when they met together. The differences they had, which are often projected as irreconcilable, need to be viewed through the lens of their calling. Paul's apostolic focal point was the Gentiles. James' apostolic focal point was the Jews.

Salvation for both people groups comes through faith in the atoning sacrifice of Jesus, God's own Son—the eternal Lamb of God. As we will see, on this point they are in full agreement.

Both James and Paul are determined to let their light shine before men (Matthew 5:16), even in the temple courts—even at the risk of their lives—even to the point of death. The violent zealotry for the law that plays out when Paul is seized, beaten, and arrested in the temple foreshadows what will ultimately happen to James a few years later. In Paul's case, a Roman commander intervened to save his life.

James was not so fortunate.

Part Three

James the Reflection of Jesus

James through the Lens of his Epistle

17

To the Twelve Tribes Scattered among the Nations

We can learn a great deal about James through the Gospels, through the Book of Acts, and through Paul's references to him in his epistles. But ultimately the character of the reborn James is most eloquently revealed through his own writing—through his epistle, the Epistle of James.

Biblical scholars are divided when assigning a date for when the Epistle of James was written. It can be no later than 62 AD, since Josephus indicates that was the year when James was martyred. There is some evidence that it may have been written in the forties, and if true, it would then predate Paul's letters. William Varner is among the scholars who favor an earlier date.[129] In his notes on James, K. Arthur also situates the epistle "sometime before 50 A.D. or in the early A.D. 50s."[130] R.V.G Tasker places the most likely date as about AD 60.

In his introduction to the epistle of James, Jon Mark Ruthven states, "We cannot be dogmatic, and can only conclude that the letter was written between AD 48 and 62."[131]

---

[129] William Varner, *James Evangelical Exegetical Commentary* (Lexham, 2014), p.17.

[130] Arthur, *The International Inductive Study New Testament*, p. 355.

[131] Ruthven, "Introduction: James," *Spirit Filled Life Bible,* p. 1893.

William Varner's early date seems improbable, since it comes before the Council of Jerusalem in AD 50 that welcomed the Gentiles into the fellowship of the church. However, a date in the early AD 50s or earlier is intriguing because it raises several questions.

Is the Epistle of James the first epistle in the canon? Did James set the pattern or standard for the other canonical epistle writers? Were Paul, Peter, John, and Jude following the example of James when they picked up the quill pen and wrote their epistles to local churches or more broadly to the universal church? Or alternately was James following the example of Paul when he wrote his epistle?

Due to James' leadership role in the church, as demonstrated at the Council of Jerusalem, it is not unreasonable to surmise that he may also have led the way in addressing the rapidly growing church through this Holy Spirit inspired literary form.

In fact, James had ample reasons to write an epistle. Having opened the door of the church to uncircumcised believers, he had a responsibility to ensure that these new converts were fully acquainted with the teaching and ethics of their Lord and Savior. Having put their faith in Jesus, how should these new believers live? With his practical, direct approach James answers that question in his epistle.

Furthermore, through his friendship with Paul and by his endorsement of his ministry, James had an envoy through whom he could ensure that his epistle was widely read throughout Paul's network of churches.

As Ruthven states, we cannot be dogmatic on these points, but through James and Paul's interaction we can see there is a logical progression that can readily explain the development of the epistles as a New Testament form of inter-church communication and teaching. James and his epistle sit at the heart of this first-century inter-church dialogue.

The Epistle of James appears in our bibles as the first of what are commonly called the general epistles. These epistles are called general because they are not addressed to a specific congregation, such as the church in Corinth or Ephesus.

But James does have an audience that he addresses with his greeting:

From James, a servant of God and of our Lord Jesus
Christ.

Greetings to the twelve tribes scattered all over the
world. (James 1:1, CEV)

There is a humility in James' self-introduction that is worthy of
comment. He does not identify himself as the brother of Jesus; to do so
would be self-exalting. Instead, he simply identifies as *"a servant of God
and of our Lord Jesus Christ."*

By identifying himself as a servant, James is accurately reflecting
the character of his brother, who continually identified himself as a
servant. On his final night with his disciples, Jesus assumed a servant's
role as he stooped to wash their feet (John 13:2-17). Now in his role
as overseer, James addresses the church of Jesus Christ as the Lord's
humble servant.

By declining to identify himself as Jesus' brother, James is following
the pattern of humility and self-effacement exemplified by his brother.
Though Jesus was the Son of God, he did not refer to himself in those
terms. He preferred the term 'son of man.' Even in his trial before the
Jewish High Council, when he was directly asked if he was the Son of
God, he answered, *"You say that I am."* (Luke 22:70)

James takes the same approach as his brother. Rather than self-iden-
tify as the brother of Jesus, he allows others to identify him as such. He
assumes a humble position. James refuses to take the place of honor
until he is asked to do so, just as Jesus taught in one of his parables about
guests arriving at a banquet (Luke 14:7–11).

James' letter is addressed to *"the twelve tribes scattered all over the
world"* (CEV) or as the more traditional King James Version reads *"to the
twelve tribes which are scattered abroad."* At first glance one might assume
that this means that James is writing exclusively to the Jewish diaspora.
Some Bible scholars interpret this phrase in this narrow, literal sense.
But there is ample evidence to suggest that the phrase *"twelve tribes"* is
in fact inclusive of all Christian believers regardless of race or nationality.
Under the new covenant ushered in by Jesus, followers of Christ are the
new Israel of God (Galatians 6:14–16).

Tasker sees the phrase "*twelve tribes*" as a symbolic description of the new Israel.

> James is not addressing a single group of Christians with whose circumstances he is familiar, but various congregations of Christians scattered far and wide throughout the Roman world. Together, these groups constitute the people of God who are continuous with the old Israel but consist of all, regardless of nationality, who acknowledge Jesus as God's Messiah.[132]

The view that the phrase "*twelve tribes scattered all over the world*" is a description of the church as the new Israel is strengthened by Peter's use of a similar phrase in 1 Peter 1:1. Peter addresses his letter to "*the exiles of the Dispersion*" (RSV) or scattering.

In the same way Paul, in his closing remarks to the largely Gentile churches of Galatia, refers to them and the global church as the "*Israel of God*" (Galatians 6:16). The point being made here is that the apostles saw all those who were redeemed by Christ as heirs of the new kingdom that he was establishing. This new kingdom is the "*Israel of God*" which James metaphorically calls the "*twelve tribes*" of the dispersion. According to Paul, the new converts are all the children of Abraham by faith.[133] Thus, it includes all the redeemed who have put their faith in Jesus Christ, both Jew and Gentile.

It logically follows that the Epistle of James is addressed to Christian believers everywhere and for all time. The scattering or dispersion of believers throughout the world, whether through persecution or missionary endeavor, alludes to Jesus' teaching about the growth of the kingdom of God as he compares it to yeast in a lump of dough (Matthew 13:33).

In the same vein, in the week prior to his death, Jesus taught via his Parable of the Tenants that a sharp change was coming (Matthew 21:33–46). He spoke this prophetic warning to the chief priests and

---

[132] R.V.G. Tasker, *The General Epistle of James: An Introduction and Commentary—Tyndale New Testament Commentaries* (Eerdmans, 1983), p. 39.

[133] "*Understand, then, that those who have faith are children of Abraham*" (Galatians 3:7).

Pharisees: "Therefore I tell you that the kingdom of God will be taken away from you and given to a people who will produce its fruit" (Matthew 21:43).

The kingdom of God was being transferred from the Jewish nation to those who accepted the rulership of Jesus, the Messiah king. Christ's dire warning had its fulfillment with the destruction of Jerusalem in 70 AD and the exile of the Jewish population from their homeland. Much of Jesus' discourse in Matthew 24 predicts and describes this traumatic national event.

Paul points out that by God's grace and through the message of the gospel, Jews and Gentiles are being drawn together in one body.

> In reading this, then, you will be able to understand my insight into the mystery of Christ, which was not made known to people in other generations as it has now been revealed by the Spirit to God's holy apostles and prophets. This mystery is that through the gospel the Gentiles are heirs together with Israel, members together of one body, and sharers together in the promise in Christ Jesus. (Ephesians 3:4–6)

With the opening salutation of his epistle, then, James was tapping into the great mystery of the gospel, which binds Jews and Gentiles together as one people through faith in Christ Jesus. He was writing to a dispersed and culturally diverse church he had explicitly authorized by his decision at the Council of Jerusalem.

And how did one become a citizen of the kingdom of God and member of the church of Christ? James provides the answer in the first chapter of his epistle.

> Don't be deceived, my dear brothers and sisters. Every good and perfect gift is from above, coming down from the Father of the heavenly lights, who does not change like shifting shadows. He chose to give us

birth through the word of truth, that we might be a
kind of firstfruits of all he created. (James 1:16–18)

With this brief statement James encapsulates the core gospel message. Salvation is a gift[134] from our gracious heavenly Father who has
chosen us[135] and given us new birth into His family through the Word,[136]
which came to us in human flesh in the person of Jesus.[137] In short, we
become citizens of the kingdom through rebirth, just as Jesus taught
Nicodemus in John 3.

This statement fully aligns with the teaching found throughout the
other New Testament texts. James and Paul were initially opponents of
the ministry of Christ, yet after their conversion they came into agreement on the key elements of the gospel message.

How did that alignment come about? Undoubtedly, it came about
as both men met with the apostles who were present during Jesus' active
ministry. The Twelve heard Jesus' teachings, witnessed his interactions
with the crowds, and saw his miraculous powers. One can easily imagine
James as an eager new convert meeting with Matthew, Peter, and John,
and discussing the key events and the teachings of Jesus' ministry—
events he was not present for.

With the passage of time, it became ever more urgent that these
oral accounts be recorded for posterity. In his leadership role, did James
by word or by the example provided by his epistle encourage the gospel writers to record the events they witnessed and researched? Possibly.
What is clear is that through his epistle, James conveys the ethos, character, and spirit of his brother Jesus.

In summary, James 1:16-18 establishes the apostolic orthodoxy of
James' understanding of the gospel, and James 1:1 establishes the uni-
versality of the audience for his message. Now let's dig deeper and consider the scope and content of his epistle.

---

[134] Ephesians 2:8–9.

[135] 1 Peter 1:1–2.

[136] *For you have been born again, not of perishable seed, but of imperishable, through the
living and enduring word of God* (1 Peter 1:23).

[137] John 1:1–5, John 1:9–13.

—— 18 ——

James–More than an Epistle of Straw

There is something quite unique about the Epistle of James. It does not easily fit into the pattern of the other apostolic writings. There is a sharpness—a directness—that many readers find both challenging and refreshing.

In his writing James goes for the jugular with the relentless precision of an attack dog. And what is he attacking? He is attacking the hypocrisy, lethargy, and complacency that can so easily set into a believer's life.

When the epistle is read in its entirety, the reader may come away with a keen desire to repent. It is an epistle that demands change—that requires action—that convicts the wayward.

If you are looking for comfort, you won't find it in the Epistle of James. If you are looking for a philosophical discussion on the merits of the gospel or a treatise on various doctrinal points, you won't find that either. What you do find is an unequivocal call for right living. For practical-minded James, wisdom is not an intellectual exercise. Wisdom must be expressed through right words and actions.

> Are any of you wise or sensible? Then show it by living right and by being humble and wise in everything you do. But if your heart is full of bitter jealousy and selfishness, don't brag or lie to cover up the truth. That

kind of wisdom doesn't come from above. It is earthly and selfish and comes from the devil himself. Whenever people are jealous or selfish, they cause trouble and do all sorts of cruel things. But the wisdom that comes from above leads us to be pure, friendly, gentle, sensible, kind, helpful, genuine, and sincere. When peacemakers plant seeds of peace, they will harvest justice. (James 3:13–18, CEV)

An appeal for humility, right living, and bold faith are at the core of this epistle.

Jon Mark Ruthven makes these observations on James' purpose for writing the Epistle of James:

[The Epistle of] James is primarily practical and ethical, emphasizing duty rather than doctrine. The author wrote to rebuke the shameful neglect of certain Christian duties. In doing so, he analyzed the nature of genuine faith and urged his readers to demonstrate the validity of their experience with Christ. His supreme concern was reality in religion, and he set forth the practical claims of the gospel.[138]

It is the uniqueness of the Epistle of James that led to the near rejection of this book from the canon of scripture in the sixteenth century. No other book of the New Testament has such a laser-like focus on right living. To be clear, the Epistle of James was readily accepted by the early church fathers and was authoritatively quoted by Origen in the first half of the third century.

According to R.V.G. Tasker, "the Epistle of James had become firmly established in the canon of the western part of Christendom by the end of the fourth century."[139]

---

[138] Ruthven, "Introduction: James," *Spirit Filled Life Bible,* p. 1893.

[139] R.V.G. Tasker, *The General Epistle of James: An Introduction and Commentary—Tyndale New Testament Commentaries* (Eerdmans, 1983), p. 17.

But the early reformers and Luther in particular had little use for the Epistle of James. Luther considered the letter an "epistle of straw," since it lacked the doctrinal heft of the other epistles. He relegated the epistle to the back of his German translation of the New Testament because, among other things, he doubted that it was actually authored by James.

Citing J.H. Ropes, Tasker asserts that Erasmus and Luther "ascribed the letter to 'some good, pious man who had taken some sayings from the apostle's disciples.'"[140]

But Martin Luther's problems with Epistle of James ran much deeper than uncertainty about the book's authorship. Luther objected to one of the central tenets of James' epistle. James boldly asserted that "*faith without works is dead.*"

> My friends, what good is it to say you have faith, when you don't do anything to show that you really do have faith? Can that kind of faith save you? If you know someone who doesn't have any clothes or food, you shouldn't just say, "I hope all goes well for you. I hope you will be warm and have plenty to eat." What good is it to say this, unless you do something to help? Faith that doesn't lead us to do good deeds is all alone and dead!
>
> Suppose someone disagrees and says, "It is possible to have faith without doing kind deeds."
>
> I would answer, "Prove that you have faith without doing kind deeds, and I will prove that I have faith by doing them." You surely believe there is only one God. That's fine. Even demons believe this, and it makes them shake with fear.
>
> Does some stupid person want proof that faith without deeds is useless? Well, our ancestor Abraham pleased God by putting his son Isaac on the altar to sacrifice him. Now you see how Abraham's faith and deeds

---

[140] Tasker, *The General Epistle of James*, p. 21.

worked together. He proved that his faith was real by what he did. This is what the Scriptures mean by saying, "Abraham had faith in God, and God was pleased with him." That's how Abraham became God's friend.

You can now see that we please God by what we do and not only by what we believe. For example, Rahab had been a prostitute. But she pleased God when she welcomed the spies and sent them home by another way.

Anyone who doesn't breathe is dead, and faith that doesn't do anything is just as dead! (James 2:14–26, CEV)

Luther had ushered in the Reformation on the doctrine of salvation by faith alone—*sola fide*. He had staked his faith and actions on the writings of Paul, which clearly stated that salvation came as a result of grace through faith and not of works.

We who are Jews by birth and not sinful Gentiles know that a person is not justified by the works of the law, but by faith in Jesus Christ. So we, too, have put our faith in Christ Jesus that we may be justified by faith in Christ and not by the works of the law, because by the works of the law no one will be justified. (Galatians 2:15–16, NIV)

For Luther the Epistle of James represented a clear contradiction of his interpretation of the passage above from Galatians, and other passages from Paul's epistles such as Ephesians 2:4–8 and Romans 5:1–2. James' letter placed great emphasis on right living, while Paul's letters emphasized the rightness of faith in Christ.

Under Luther's leadership, justification before God by grace through faith became the central theme of the Reformation. Works had no part to play in personal salvation, since salvation was not earned. It came as a gift by God's grace. But with statements such as, "*As the body without the spirit is dead, so faith without deeds is dead*" (James 2:26, NIV), James appeared to contradict the central tenet on which Luther's understanding of faith was built. The Epistle of James appeared to undermine the founding premise of the entire Reformation.

Rather than reconcile these apparent doctrinal contradictions between two beloved apostles, Luther discounted James as an epistle of straw and shuffled it off to the back of his translation of the Bible—along with what he considered to be other low value books, such as Hebrews, Jude, and Revelation.

Tasker makes the following assessment:

> He [Luther] had arbitrarily, and without any support from ancient manuscripts, placed the four books which he considered to be of doubtful apostolic authority and of secondary value doctrinally at the end of the New Testament published in 1522, to form a kind of supplement; and he did not number them in the table of contents.[141]

So, what exactly did Luther say about the Epistle of James? In context, here is J. H. Ropes' translation from German of his 1522 words:

> In fine, Saint John's Gospel and in his first Epistle, Saint Paul's epistles, especially those to the Romans, Galatians and Ephesians, and Saint Peter's first epistle—these are the books which show thee Christ, and teach thee everything that is needful and blessed for thee to know even though thou never see or hear any other book or doctrine. Therefore is Saint James's epistle a right strawy epistle in comparison with them, for it has no gospel character to it.[142]

---

[141] Tasker, *The General Epistle of James*, p. 13.

[142] James Hardy Ropes, *A Critical and Exegetical Commentary on the Epistle of St. James* (Clark, 1916), p. 106.

The impact of this negative assessment of James' epistle has rippled down through centuries. It has also colored our perspective of the person of James. He has been viewed as a theological lightweight beside the likes of Peter and Paul. But is this a fair and accurate assessment?

History has not been kind to James. Although James played a prominent and pivotal role in the first-century church, his role and his theological significance has largely been ignored, downplayed, or misunderstood down through the ages.

In the medieval period, the Roman Catholic Church drifted into what many reformers would call an idolatrous worship of Mary. This exaltation of Mary was matched with the development of several doctrinal positions which find no basis in scripture. These include the doctrine of the immaculate conception of Mary, her perpetual virginity, and her bodily assumption into heaven.

The doctrine of the perpetual virginity of Mary is particularly troublesome when it comes to our understanding of James, since it strips him of his lineage and his direct brotherhood with Jesus. Thus emasculated, his words and life story lack the rightful authority and gravitas that this direct link to Christ confers.

With the emergence of the Reformation, with its emphasis on the centrality of the holy scriptures, it would only seem logical that James would regain the recognition he deserved. But alas, this was not the case. Luther found James' epistle wanting because he viewed it as undermining the doctrine of *sola fide*.

Furthermore, Roman Catholic theologians drew comfort from the Epistle of James because in it they found the basis for two sacraments: the sacrament of divine unction (anointing the sick with oil for healing), and the sacrament of confession to the parish priest. Luther rejected both as sacraments of the church.

Though the early reformers recognized James' lineage as the half-brother of Jesus, they found his theology suspect, since it appeared to contradict the writings of Paul. They believed, the Epistle of James appeared to undercut one of the foundational truths of the Reformation, namely the doctrine of justification by faith.

With the dawn of the Reformation, a great rift emerged in Christendom, which led to the formation of the various Protestant churches. The Epistle of James lies right at the heart of that fault line. Catholicism embraced a more works-oriented path to salvation—a path apparently endorsed by James—while Protestantism embraced salvation by grace through faith—a path endorsed by Paul.

These opposing positions led to war and upheaval in Europe on a massive scale. All this is beyond strange when we consider that in their lifetime, according to the scriptures, Paul and James got along very well. They collaborated, respected one another, and each admired the other's gifting and calling. Now some 1,500 later, Christians were killing one another in an argument over letters that these two friends had written.

Since the Reformation, some theologians would have us believe that these two men were at loggerheads, each with their doctrinal daggers drawn. As we have seen in earlier chapters, by examining their relationship through the lens of scripture, there is no basis for such an argument. Despite having strongly held views and differing spheres of influence—Paul among the Gentile converts and James among Jewish converts—both were able to work with one another for the common good of the church.

So, are the theological differences between James and Paul more apparent than real? There certainly are several reasons to believe this is the case.

The first argument for a theological reconciliation between Paul and James has already been made. There is no evidence of relational conflict between Paul and James. Doctrinal conflict frequently leads to relational conflict, but the scripture provides us with no smoking gun in this regard. Texts written by Luke and Paul and the quoted words of James indicate a strong, healthy relationship between these two leaders.

Secondly, when examining a piece of writing, one needs to consider the author's purpose. In his epistle, James was not writing with the purpose of laying out a theological framework for salvation, as was the case with Paul's epistle to the Romans. James was writing an appeal to believers for righteous living. Much of Luther's criticism of the Epistle of James is unwarranted. James is being faulted for what he did not write. This is like criticizing a dog for not being a cat.

Thirdly, on the surface it may appear that James and Paul are at odds on the role that faith and deeds play in salvation, but a closer examination reveals otherwise. For both Paul and James, having faith—saving faith—is not a passive response. True and saving faith is more than providing intellectual assent to a prescribed set of beliefs. That is precisely the argument that James is making when he claims that even demons believe in God, but their faith does not save them (James 2:19). For Paul as well, saving faith meant far more than intellectual assent.

Fourth, Paul and James agreed that genuine faith is personally transformative. Paul expected and called for personal transformation in the lives of every one of his converts.[143] How did that changed life reveal itself? Through deeds, of course. Time and again in his epistles, Paul calls for evidence of changed lives in the daily conduct of believers. Often these direct calls to action or works are found near the end of Paul's epistles,[144] since often he begins his letters by dealing with specific problems that have arisen in the church, or by presenting foundational truths of the Christian faith.

James expected and called for personal transformation as well, but his epistle represents a shift from the Pauline paradigm. His entire epistle is a call for transformative, Christ-motivated actions, attitudes, and behavior.

In his discussion of the content of the Epistle of James, Jon Mark Ruthven makes this observation:

> Rather than speculating or debating on religious theories, James directs his readers toward godly living. From the beginning to the end the mood of his letter is imperative. In 108 verses, 54 clear commands are given, and seven times James calls attention to his statements by using terms that are imperative in nature. This "bondservant of God" [James 1:1] writes as one supervising other slaves. The result is a statement

---

[143] See Ephesians 2:1–10.

[144] For examples of Paul's calls to action, see Ephesians 4:25–6:20, 1 Thessalonians 5:12–22, and Colossians 3:18–4:6.

of Christian ethics, which stands on par with any such teaching in the New Testament.[145]

Finally, one needs to consider the work of the Holy Spirit. The Holy Spirit inspired both Paul and James to write their epistles. If we believe in the divine inspiration of the holy scriptures, it then follows that these two apostles, using their skills and experiences, wrote as the Holy Spirit directed them to write.

> All Scripture is God-breathed and is useful for teaching, rebuking, correcting and training in righteousness, so that the servant of God may be thoroughly equipped for every good work. (1 Timothy 3:16–17)

From the earliest times the church has recognized the writings of James and Paul as God-breathed. If the Holy Spirit directed James to write an epistle focussed on practical Christian living, who are we question the wisdom of the Holy Spirit? Our understanding of what it means to live as a follower of Jesus would be considerably diminished without the Epistle of James.

In many respects James acts as a counterbalance to Paul. His epistle counters the notion of cheap grace that places no requirements on the believer. A hefty dose of Luther's doctrine of *sola fide* can lead to a culture of easy believe-ism and an aversion to calls for personal holiness. Within such a church culture, anything that requires effort or personal sacrifice is frowned upon because it might be misconstrued as an attempt to earn one's salvation.

In the last century, through his writing and the example he set by his life and death, the German Lutheran theologian Dietrich Bonhoeffer warned about the consequences of cheap grace—the results of which are a church rife with sin, which has no effective witness to the world because it conforms to the social and moral norms of the world. The Epistle of James is the biblical antidote to the easy believe-ism that Bonhoeffer warned against.

---

[145] Ruthven, "Introduction: James," *Spirit Filled Life Bible,* p. 1893.

Similarly, a century before Bonhoeffer, the noted theologian and philosopher Soren Kierkegaard saw the Epistle of James as his chief weapon against the hypocrisy of his day.

> It is surely both interesting and illuminating to recall that, when Soren Kierkegaard in the middle of the nineteenth century felt called to use his great gifts of eloquence and satire in a sustained warfare against the worldliness and hypocrisy of the contemporary Church, it was the Epistle of James that both inspired him for battle and supplied him with the ammunition with which to fight.[146]

It has been said that any doctrinal truth pushed to an extreme can lead to heresy. Though there is great truth in the doctrine of justification by grace through faith, when this teaching is embraced to the exclusion of other biblical truths, the result is a distortion of truth, since it does not take into account the whole counsel of the Scriptures.

Kierkegaard was keenly aware of the effects of this distortion of truth. For him, according to one of his biographers, the Epistle of James represented the ideal counterweight.

> Kierkegaard, while acknowledging the truth of Justification by Faith, as directed against "work-righteousness" and the assumption that one can earn his righteousness, had seen that the temper of the times "especially in Protestantism, and more especially in Denmark" required the proclamation of a complementary truth—a bringing to the fore of the practical, ethical side of Christianity, not by any means to the exclusion or minimizing of its dogmatic aspects, but to the exclusion of that barren orthodoxy which would make mere intellectual belief the primary act of Christian faith. The highly practical Epistle of

---

[146] Tasker, *The General Epistle of James,* pp. 10–11.

James... was and remained Kierkegaard's favourite Scripture.[147]

So, what are we to make of Luther's assessment of the Epistle of James? Through the benefits of history and hindsight, we can see that this "right strawy Epistle" was and is the perfect counterweight to the excesses of *sola fide,* when this doctrine is pushed to the extreme while ignoring the full counsel of Scripture.

Clearly Luther made an enormous contribution to our understanding of the Christian faith and his courage, determination, and hard work rescued many truths of the Bible from the dustbin of history. His translation of the Bible into the vernacular of the people unleashed a tidal wave that transformed Europe and the world. Thanks to his foundational work, people all over the world can read the Bible in their mother tongue and decide for themselves if this letter from James is an epistle of straw or an epistle filled with nuggets of pure gold.

[147] Robert Brettall, *A Kierkegaard Anthology* (Oxford University, 1947), p. 282.

199

——— 19 ———

James and Jesus–Reflecting His Brother's Voice

A few weeks ago, I had a rather embarrassing experience. My wife handed me the telephone, saying, "It's Josh." Josh is my youngest son.

For some reason my wife's comment did not register in my brain. My mind had been on my oldest son Tim. For the next five minutes, our phone conversation continued with me convinced that I was talking to Tim. It was only when some life circumstances did not align that I realized I was speaking to Josh. I felt truly embarrassed. I had trouble distinguishing between my sons' voices!

The plain truth of the matter is that brothers' voices sound similar. There is something in the genetic make-up of the vocal cords and the oral structures that result in a similar sounding voice. Audiologists will tell you that every person's voiceprint is unique, but there are vocal and speech pattern similarities within families. These develop not just because of genetics, but because they spend so much time speaking to each other.

In the same way writers have a voice. Each author has a distinctive way of writing. If you are familiar with an author's writing style, you can often identify an unfamiliar piece of his or her writing by style alone. Just as each of us has unique fingerprints and voiceprints, we also have a unique way of writing—a writing voice.

When we examine the Epistle of James, we see a writing style—syntax, word choice, and sentence structure—that is unique to James. The other New Testament epistle writers—Peter, Paul, John, and Jude—each have a unique voice, a unique way they use written language to express their ideas.

What truly sets James apart is his brotherhood with Jesus. Since Jesus and James are brothers, can we find Jesus' voice reflected in the Epistle of James? More specifically can we hear the voice, core values, and tone of Jesus through the written words of James? If these two men are really brothers, raised in the same household, exposed to the same values, then it logically follows that their voice would align in many respects.

It would seem only natural that Jesus and the regenerate James would have the same interests and ideals. Are these reflected in the Epistle of James? Is James animated by the same issues and concerns that animated the life of Jesus?

Jesus was not a writer; he has left us with no written text. Fortunately, the Gospels provide us with many direct quotations. But if Jesus wrote an epistle, would the voice in that epistle sound more like Paul or more like James? There are ample grounds to believe such an epistle would read a lot like James.

If you read the Epistle of James with your ear attuned for the voice and tone of Jesus, the epistle comes alive in a whole new way. The character of this epistle is reflective of the character of Jesus like no other piece of Christian literature.

With these questions in mind, let's examine the Epistle of James to try and find the voice of Jesus in its text. The intent is not to provide a verse-by-verse commentary on the epistle. There are several fine commentaries on the market that do just that. Instead, this chapter provides an overview of the epistle, with a focus on indicators of James' brotherhood with Jesus.

Discerning the actual structure of this epistle has been a problem for many Bible scholars. The letter appears to be series of vivid observations coupled with commands for righteous living.

Because it is filled with short, pithy sayings, some have compared the Epistle of James to the Book of Proverbs. To an extent the comparison is valid, since wisdom for living is one of James' central themes, but the epistle is much more than a collection of proverbs.

A careful reading of the Epistle of James reveals a prevailing pattern. In the first chapter James introduces a series of topics or themes. Then over the next four chapters, he returns to each of these themes again and again. It's as though he is driving in a nail. In the first chapter or occasion, this master carpenter sets the nail and gives it that initial penetrating tap, but then over the next four chapters he returns again and again to that same theme as he drives home his point.

This can be best illustrated by looking at a specific example. One of the dominant themes throughout the epistle is the injustice of the wealthy, how that contrasts with the poor, and ultimately how God will judge the rich. James introduces this theme with these words:

> Any of God's people who are poor should be glad that he thinks so highly of them. But any who are rich should be glad when God makes them humble. Rich people will disappear like wild flowers scorched by the burning heat of the sun. The flowers lose their blossoms, and their beauty is destroyed. That is how the rich will disappear, as they go about their business. (James 1:9–11, CEV)

In chapter two James touches on this theme again when he deals with how the rich should be treated when they come to a Christian meeting:

> My friends, if you have faith in our glorious Lord Jesus Christ, you won't treat some people better than others. Suppose a rich person wearing fancy clothes and a gold ring comes to one of your meetings. And suppose a poor person dressed in worn-out clothes also comes. You must not give the best seat to the one in fancy clothes and tell the one who is poor to stand at the side or sit on the floor. That is the same as saying that some

people are better than others, and you would be acting like a crooked judge.

My dear friends, pay attention. God has given a lot of faith to the poor people in this world. He has also promised them a share in his kingdom that he will give to everyone who loves him. You mistreat the poor. But isn't it the rich who boss you around and drag you off to court? Aren't they the ones who make fun of your Lord? (James 2:1–7, CEV)

Finally, in chapter five James concludes by driving the nail home with his indictment against the rich:

You rich people should cry and weep! Terrible things are going to happen to you. Your treasures have rotted and moths have eaten your clothes. Your money has rusted and the rust will be evidence against you, as it burns your body like fire. Yet you keep on storing up wealth in these last days. You refused to pay the people who worked in your fields and now their unpaid wages are shouting out against you. The Lord All-Powerful has surely heard the cries of the workers who harvested your crops.

While here on earth, you have thought only of filling your own stomachs and having a good time. But now you are like fat cattle on their way to be butchered. You have condemned and murdered innocent people, who couldn't even fight back. (James 5:1–6, CEV)

James uses the same approach as he addresses other themes or topics. He introduces the theme of faith early in his epistle with this passage:

But when you ask for something, you must have faith and not doubt. Anyone who doubts is like an ocean wave tossed around in a storm. If you are that kind of person, you can't make up your mind, and you surely can't be trusted. So don't expect the Lord to give you anything at all. (James 1:6–8, CEV)

This is followed by the major faith/works discourse already cited earlier, where he discusses and contrasts the faith of Abraham and of demons (James 2:14–26).

Then in chapter five he drives the nail of faith deeper with these words:

> If you are sick, ask the church leaders to come and pray for you. Ask them to put olive oil on you in the name of the Lord. If you have faith when you pray for sick people, they will get well. The Lord will heal them, and if they have sinned, he will forgive them. (James 5:14–15, CEV)

He delivers the final blow on this theme by using the illustration of Elijah's prayer of faith:

> The prayer of an innocent person is powerful, and it can help a lot. Elijah was just as human as we are, and for three and a half years his prayers kept the rain from falling. But when he did pray for rain, it fell from the skies and made the crops grow. (James 5:16b–18, CEV)

This pattern of introducing a theme and then returning again and again to drive it home is a feature that is unique to James' writing style. But this pattern of repetition was also used by Jesus when he was teaching. Jesus did not give us one parable about the kingdom of God. In the thirteenth chapter of Matthew, he presents seven kingdom parables in a single teaching session.

Similarly, Jesus did not tell just one story to illustrate the truth of God's love for a lost soul: he gave us three. In Luke 15 he gave us the story of the prodigal, the lost coin, and the lost sheep. This propensity for repetition, and for examining a truth from various angles, is a brotherly trait that James carried through into his writing.

Another pervasive style element that we have already touched on is James' frequent use of the imperative. Jon Mark Ruthven pointed out that there are 52 commands in the 104 verses of James' epistle. James makes far greater use of the imperative form than any other New Testament epistle writer. He writes as one having authority. This is only fitting since he served as the head of the mother church in Jerusalem.

But James' authoritative tone also reflects the tone that Jesus projected. After completing his Sermon on the Mount, Jesus drew this reaction:

> When Jesus had finished saying these things, the crowds were amazed at his teaching, because he taught as one who had authority, and not as their teachers of the law. (Matthew 7:28–29)

In this important respect, the voice of Jesus and the written voice of James are remarkably similar. Like his older brother, James calls his readers to action. There is nothing tentative or uncertain about the notes he sounds. His letter is a clarion call for right living and bold faith. As with Jesus, it's this boldness that demands respect.

Here is a list of the major themes that James sequentially drives home with this authoritative writing style:

- Perseverance during times of testing (James 1:2–4, 1:12, 5:7–11)
- Wisdom for living right (James 1:5, 3:13–18)
- Faith applied in action and prayer (James 1:6–8, 1:27, 2:14–26, 5:14–18)
- Controlling the tongue (James 1:19–21, 1:26, 3:1–12, 4:11–12, 5:12)
- The injustice of wealth and poverty (James 1:9–11, 2:1–7, 5:1–6)
- Overcoming temptation (James 1:12–15, 4:1–9, 4:17, 5:16)
- The need for humility (James 1:21, 3:13, 4:6–10)

- Obeying God's word (James 1:22–25, 2:8–13)
- The Lord's return and eternal judgement (James 1:12, 2:12–13, 4:11–12, 5:7–9)
- Repentance and confession (James 4:7–9, 5:16)
- God's opposition to pride and boasting (James 4:6, 4:13–17)

Some of these themes overlap and are interconnected as James builds his argument for right living by putting practical Christian faith into action. As he addresses each theme, this master carpenter is building a house on the solid rock of Christ's teachings (Matthew 7:24–27).

Many commentators on the Epistle of James have noted a striking similarity in the style and content of this epistle and Jesus' Sermon on the Mount. In particular, the epistle reflects the values set forth in the Beatitudes.

Adding credence to this position, Tasker provides us with this observation:

> The authorship of James the brother of the Lord is not only consonant with the note of authority which sounds throughout the epistle, and with the possible echoes of the speech of James at the council of Jerusalem, but also with the extent to which the writer has obviously been profoundly impressed by the teaching of Jesus as we know it today in the Sermon on the Mount.[148]

An author—any author—begins with a blank page, but what he chooses to write reflects his character and the thinking and values that occupy his mind. Keeping this statement in mind, why did James choose to focus on the major themes that he selected for his epistle?

It appears that he chose these themes because they were at the heart of Jesus' teachings. As Tasker states, in his thinking James was "profoundly impressed by the teaching of Jesus." Every aspect of his epistle reflects this.

---

[148] Tasker, *The General Epistle of James*, p. 28.

Why does James identify himself with the poor and heap condemnation on the rich? Because Jesus did just that. The first Beatitude is *"Blessed are the poor in spirit, for theirs is the kingdom of heaven"* (Matthew 5:3). Throughout his ministry, Jesus identified with the poor and took a skewer to the rich and powerful. His story of the rich man and Lazarus is a fine example of this (Luke 16:19–31).

James' attack on the excesses and injustice of the wealthy in James 5:1-6 bears a remarkable resemblance to Jesus' attack on the hypocrisy of the Pharisees and teachers of the law in Matthew 23. The tone is virtually identical. None of the other New Testament writers take such a direct and confrontational approach. Furthermore, it is hard to ignore the current relevance of James' words. With the world economy dominated and controlled by oligarchs and corporate greed, James pens an indictment worthy of his older brother.

Why does James define faith as he does? Why is his definition linked with actions? Again, Jesus defined faith in terms of actions or deeds. In every instance where Jesus called for faith, he was not expecting mere intellectual acknowledgement. For Jesus faith is directly linked to words and actions.

When the tax collector Zacchaeus repents, Jesus declares, *"Today salvation has come to this house, because this man, too, is a son of Abraham"* (Luke 19:9). He makes this statement after Zacchaeus announces, *"Look, Lord! Here and now I give half of my possessions to the poor, and if I have cheated anybody out of anything, I will pay back four times the amount"* (Luke 19:8). For Jesus faith, deeds, and salvation form a seamless whole.

The Pauline approach to faith, deeds, and salvation is quite different. Faith, deeds, and salvation are treated as separate entities or components of a believer's life experience. For Jesus and James these form a single package. For these brothers, faith, deeds, and salvation are integral to one another.

For both James and Jesus, active faith is not only called for but expected. Jesus repeatedly upbraided his disciples for their lack of faith. James exhibits the same character trait. He has the same high expectation of his readers.

But when you ask for something, you must have faith and not doubt. Anyone who doubts is like an ocean wave tossed around in a storm. If you are that kind of person, you can't make up your mind, and you surely can't be trusted. So don't expect the Lord to give you anything at all. (James 1:6–8, CEV)

The words of James on this topic run parallel to the words of Jesus:

Therefore I tell you, whatever you ask for in prayer, believe that you have received it, and it will be yours. (Mark 11:24)

There is no room for doubt in the brothers' approach to faith. They demand a full throttle commitment. James asserts, "*The prayer offered in faith will make the sick person well; the Lord will raise them up*" (James 5:15). There is no hesitation or equivocating in that statement. Faith will bring results. Bold, audacious faith brought results in Jesus' ministry—and James leaves no room for doubt that a similar application of faith brought the same results in his own ministry. Furthermore, he expects results from his readers as they exercise their faith by heeding his words.

Words—yes, words—are at the very core of faith and life for these two men. The power of the tongue for good or evil is central to the Epistle of James. Perhaps no author has harnessed the written word quite as effectively as James in describing the havoc inflicted by the tongue. (See James 3:1–12.)

In his condemnation of the restless tongue, James was simply reflecting the words and thoughts of his brother:

You brood of vipers, how can you who are evil say anything good? For the mouth speaks what the heart is full of. A good man brings good things out of the good stored up in him, and an evil man brings evil things out of the evil stored up in him. (Matthew 12:34–35)

Again, this theme of the power of the tongue is central to James' epistle because it was central to Jesus' ministry. In his Sermon on the Mount, Jesus insisted that his followers not swear oaths. He taught, "*All you need to say is simply 'Yes' or 'No'; anything beyond this comes from the evil one*" (Matthew 5:33–37). James essentially repeats the same admonition in James 5:12.

This profound emphasis on the spoken word is only fitting, since according to the scriptures Jesus is the living Word. He is the Word—the spoken Word—by which the heavens and the earth were formed (John 1:1-5). In his earthly ministry, he brought sight to the blind, hearing to the deaf, and health to the crippled body with a word. With his words he brought forgiveness and spiritual rebirth.

James affirms that the born-again experience comes through the word: "*He chose to give us birth through the word of truth, that we might be a kind of firstfruits of all he created*" (James 1:18).

It's the power of the "*word of truth*" that James is lifting up throughout his epistle. He does that most effectively by systematically focusing on the core teachings of Jesus, as recorded in the Sermon on the Mount.

How can the "*word of truth*" be exalted by believers who have a careless or malicious tongue? That would be impossible, so James methodically builds his case for self-control of that most unruly member of the body.

On the flip side, though the tongue can be destructive, it also has creative power when it comes under the influence of God. As James points out, the prayer of faith can heal the sick. In addition, he states, "*The prayer of a righteous person is powerful and effective*" (James 5:16). It logically follows that when that most unruly member is tamed and harnessed by the Lord, great things are possible.

So then, if Jesus sent a letter to the church, how would that epistle read? There are many reasons to believe such an epistle would sound a lot like the Epistle of James. This would be so because James patterned his letter on the teachings of Jesus, and because James understood and knew his brother intimately, like no other man.

The voice and tone of Jesus are heard throughout this epistle because when the resurrected Christ broke through to the stubborn heart of James, the transformation made James even more like his brother. The brothers sound alike, because they are alike.

With his conversion James took on the character of Christ. Through his epistle he urges us to do the same.

Epilogue

The Tipping Point

James – His Death and Legacy

After Paul gives his mission report before James and the elders in Acts 21, one of the elders (possibly James) makes a statement that hints at the growing power and influence of the church in Jerusalem:

> When they heard this, they praised God. Then they said to Paul: "You see, brother, how many thousands of Jews have believed, and all of them are zealous for the law." (Acts 21:20)

Scholars are divided about the size and influence of the Jewish church prior to the sacking of Jerusalem and the destruction of the temple by the Romans in AD 70. In addition to Luke's account in Acts, there is a growing body of evidence from the historical record that suggests the Jewish church was reaching a cultural or religious tipping point. That would mean the growth in the numbers of adherents was so significant it was possible to imagine Christianity becoming the dominant belief system right in heart of Judaism.

Historically, the possibility of an outbreak of persecution increases significantly when the rapid growth of Christianity approaches a tipping point within a previously homogeneous culture. This was the case in Japan when the warrior general Toyotomi Hideyoshi unleashed a wave of persecution. On February 5, 1597, he ordered the crucifixion of twenty-six Christians in Nagasaki to discourage conversions, which were becoming increasingly common. By the late 1500s Christianity in Japan was reaching a tipping point. Martyrdom and slaughter stopped the spread of Christianity in its tracks.

Currently, much of Boko Haram's persecution of Christians in northern Nigeria can be seen as a backlash against the rapid growth of the faith in that predominantly Muslim region during recent decades.

For the church in Jerusalem, severe persecution after the martyrdom of Stephen was followed by a period of relative peace due to the conversion of their chief antagonist Saul of Tarsus. For roughly two decades there was an uneasy peace between the two camps. But the growth of Christianity among the Jewish diaspora did not sit well with Jewish religious authorities. Similarly, the churches' inclusion of Gentile converts in the faith raised the ire of Jewish religious purists. The riot surrounding Paul's arrest in the temple courts was proof of that.

High taxes and unrest with Rome only compounded the religious tension. Religious zealots resisted paying taxes since Roman coinage was offensive to them.

> Roman coins had pictures of their goddess Roma or their divine emperor, which broke Jewish religious strictures against graven images and paying tribute to other gods. To make matters worse, the procurators who collected these impossible sums (Pontius Pilate was one) were in the main corrupt men who despised Jews.[149]

It appears that a tipping point was reached with the election of the new high priest Ananus. Ananus found an ideal opportunity to act against James, this troubling thorn in his side.

---

[149] Joseph Cummins, *Why Some Wars Never End: The Stories of the Longest Conflicts in History* (Fair Winds, 2010), p. 85.

According to the Jewish historian Josephus, writing ca. 94, James with "certain others" was stoned in 62 at the instigation of the Sadducee high priest Ananus, as one of his first acts as high priest. Ananus was able to carry out the execution because the newly appointed Roman procurator, Albinius, had not arrived yet in Palestine.[150]

There is no scriptural account of the death of James. What knowledge we have comes from church tradition and relies heavily on two sources, the writings of Josephus noted above and Hegesippus. Hegesippus provides more of a plot line to this story.

According to Hegesippus, James met his death after being presented to the people at Passover to give his impartial judgment about Jesus. When he proclaimed Jesus as the Son of man, seated at God' right hand, he was cast down from the temple, stoned and clubbed to death.[151]

There is something darkly fitting about the death of James. He died as his brother died:

• at the Passover
• with great brutality
• at the instigation of the high priest
• giving testimony to the divinity of Christ
• and according Hegesippus, asking for the forgiveness of his murderers.

The plot hatched by Ananus seems fitting as well. The plan was to lure James to the pinnacle of the temple so he could address the Passover crowd below. Surely the high priest knew that rather than deny

---

[150] W. A. Beardslee, *James, The Interpreter's Dictionary of the Bible, Volume 2*, Edited by George Arthur Buttrick (Abingdon, 1984), p. 793.

[151] Beardslee, *James, The Interpreter's Dictionary of the Bible, Volume 2*, pp. 793–794.

his brother's Messianic call, James would endorse him. He surely knew that James would find it difficult to resist an opportunity to testify to all gathered there that Jesus was the Christ.

All Ananus needed to do was to ensure that he had some conveniently placed henchmen in place to throw James off the wall and others of like persuasion below to guarantee his death. All proceeded exactly as planned—except the victim survived the fall. Those below made sure death came quickly.

The plot as described here bears some resemblance to an earlier plot hatched in cooperation with the Sanhedrin to have Paul murdered before he could provide a second round of testimony. This occurred after his arrest in the temple.

> The next morning some Jews formed a conspiracy and bound themselves with an oath not to eat or drink until they had killed Paul. More than forty men were involved in this plot. They went to the chief priests and the elders and said, "We have taken a solemn oath not to eat anything until we have killed Paul. Now then, you and the Sanhedrin petition the commander to bring him before you on the pretext of wanting more accurate information about his case. We are ready to kill him before he gets here." (Acts 23:12–15)

In Paul's case the plot was discovered in advance. The commander of the Roman garrison intervened by sending Paul at night and under heavy guard to Caesarea. Thanks to this Roman intervention, Paul's life was spared.

But for James, whether by a stroke of good luck or through strategic planning, Ananus was able to ensure that the Roman authorities could not intervene in this bit of dirty business—since, as Josephus points out, the procurator Albinius had not yet arrived.

On this earlier occasion Paul's life was spared, but four years later James was not so fortunate.

So, what became of the body of James? Again, from Hegesippus we read:

> And so he suffered martyrdom; and they buried him on the spot, and the pillar erected to his memory still remains, close by the temple. This man was a true witness to both Jews and Greeks that Jesus is the Christ.[152]

If this report is to be believed (and there are grounds for doubt) then it brings into question the legitimacy of the stone ossuary discovered in 2002. With the destruction of Jerusalem and the temple in AD 70, the location of this burial spot and the memorial pillar are impossible to verify.

Roman Catholics would have us believe that the bones of James are buried at the cathedral in Santiago de Compostela in northern Spain. According to one Catholic tradition, his bones were brought there by boat after his death. Despite the popularity of the pilgrimage route known as Camino de Santiago, or the Way of James, the evidence of the historic James having any actual connection to this site is scant to nonexistent. The connection of James to Spain appears to belong to the realm of medieval myth and superstition.

If Christian believers collected James' body after he was stoned, his bones may have ended up in a stone ossuary, since this was the burial practice during this historic period. Was it the stone ossuary currently belonging to Oded Golan? The verdict on that matter remains uncertain.

In 2012, after a trial lasting seven years, Oded Golan was acquitted of forging biblical artifacts. According to the trial judge's verdict, as reported in the *Times of Israel,* there was insufficient scientific evidence to validate or disprove the authenticity of the ossuary.

> In his ruling Wednesday, the judge went out of his way to say that the fact Golan had been found not guilty did not mean the artifacts were real.

---

[152] Fragments from the *Acts of the Church; Concerning the Martyrdom of James, the Brother of the Lord*, from Book 5.

His decision to clear Golan of forging the inscription on the James ossuary, he wrote, "does not mean that the inscription on the ossuary is authentic or that it was written 2,000 years ago. This will continue to be studied by scientists and archaeologists, and time will tell.

"Moreover," he wrote, "it was not proven in any way that the words 'the brother of Jesus' necessarily refer to the 'Jesus' who appears in Christian writings."

This applies to all of the artifacts in question, he added several hundred pages later in the lengthy text of his decision: "All that has been established is that the tools and the science currently at the disposal of the experts who testified were not sufficient to prove the alleged forgeries beyond a reasonable doubt as is required by criminal law."[153]

What is clear from the verdict is that uncertainty remains. This line from the judge's ruling is particularly revealing: "This will continue to be studied by scientists and archaeologists, and time will tell."

In other words, further developments or research may yet confirm that the ossuary is linked to James the brother of Jesus. Of course, just the opposite may also occur. In short, the mystery remains.

What time has told us over the centuries is that James, whether in life or death, can generate a great deal of controversy and debate. We can be certain he will continue to inspire debate.

As for the legacy of James, after centuries of neglect there has been a revival of interest in this prominent New Testament figure. The life of James—the saint, the apostle, and the hinge to the Gentile world—is being studied and re-examined as never before. New books on his life and commentaries on his epistle are appearing. The church and the world are discovering the prominent—even preeminent—role that he played in the first century church.

---

[153] Matti Friedman, "Oded Golan is not guilty of Forgery. So is the 'James Ossuary' for real?" *The Times of Israel*, (March 14, 2012).

Some of this interest comes from a renewed interest in discovering the Jewish roots of Christianity. At the same time, there has been a resurgence of Messianic Judaism in recent decades. As the first leader of the Jewish church, James quite naturally is a subject of great interest.

Finally, many scholars are discovering a deeper understanding of the Epistle of James. After centuries of denominational dogmatism, present-day theologians are discovering how James contributes to our understanding of faith and salvation. They are seeing direct links between this epistle and the central teachings of Jesus from the Sermon on the Mount.

Yet one question remains: How is James, the brother of Jesus, the lynchpin of our faith?

For the answer to that question, we need to turn to a present-day farmer with a ninety-thousand-dollar tractor. That farmer knows everything on that new tractor can work perfectly, but the tractor is useless without a lynchpin. This is because the tractor is specifically designed to pull a myriad of farm implements—such as a seeder, a plow, a hay baler, and a variety of harvest equipment. A single lynchpin is needed to hitch the tractor to all those machines. A lynchpin is not optional. It's essential.

The gospel message is like that powerful tractor. The gospel can accomplish great things—but the soil needs to be cultivated, the seed needs to be planted, and the harvest needs to be brought in. Jesus used similar agricultural analogies in many of his kingdom parables. In the first-century church, James was the lynchpin in our faith that made all this possible.

How so you ask?

First, James verifies the truth of the resurrection far more effectively than anyone else. This brother—this close family member—had publicly opposed Jesus and his message. Then suddenly, after Jesus' humiliating death as a blasphemous criminal, James flips. He testifies that Jesus is alive. He confesses his error and joins the apostles. This is an astonishing reversal that signals a transformative encounter with the resurrected Christ.

Second, James validates the truth of the born-again experience. This man who thought Christ was a lunatic suddenly changes. He embraces the faith he once mocked, joins the fellowship of believers, and is transformed by the gracious work of the Holy Spirit.

Third, James fully exemplifies the forgiveness and reconciliation embedded in the gospel message. After years of tension and animosity two brothers are fully reconciled. Where there was hate, love reigns.

Fourth—and most importantly—James throws open the door to the Gentile world for the gospel message. Intuitively he knows that this is what Jesus wants and what the scriptures predicted would happen.

Fifth, in his epistle, James declares a gospel message that works—a message that affirms the grace of God and challenges every believer to live a life of humility and service to others. James has a faith that is more than mental assent to a set of beliefs. It's a call to practical love and action.

In all these ways James acts as the lynchpin for the gospel message. He secures the message so it can penetrate the hard soil of human hearts. He releases the seed of the word into the Gentile world, and he sees an abundant harvest through men like Paul. He ensures that the message preached is balanced, practical, and a true reflection of Jesus' teaching. He was the sound leader the church needed. James was and is the essential lynchpin of our faith, who jumpstarted the first-century church.

After nearly two millennia of misinformation and neglect, James may finally be getting the respect he is due.

The stone box is empty. There are no bones in the ossuary, just as there are no bones in Jesus' tomb. When the women came to the empty tomb at the dawning of the first Sunday of a new age, they were greeted by two angels who said, "*Why do you look for the living among the dead? He is not here; he has risen!*" (See Luke 24:5-6).

When we go looking for James, we too may discover that he is not among the dead. The Christian believer knows that along with Jesus, his brother James is smiling down from glory as he enjoys all the fuss an ancient stone box has stirred up.

Appendix

A Complete List of New Testament References to James

"Isn't this the carpenter's son? Isn't his mother's name Mary, and aren't his brothers James, Joseph, Simon and Judas?" (Matthew 13:55)

Among them were Mary Magdalene, Mary the mother of James and Joseph, and the mother of Zebedee's sons. (Matthew 27:56)

Isn't this the carpenter? Isn't this Mary's son and the brother of James, Joseph, Judas and Simon? Aren't his sisters here with us?" And they took offense at him. (Mark 6:3)

Some women were watching from a distance. Among them were Mary Magdalene, Mary the mother of James the younger and of Joseph, and Salome. (Mark 15:40)

It was Mary Magdalene, Joanna, Mary the mother of James, and the others with them who told this to the apostles. (Luke 24:10)

When they arrived, they went upstairs to the room where they were staying. Those present were Peter, John, James and Andrew; Philip and Thomas, Bartholomew and Matthew; James son of Alphaeus and Simon the Zealot, and Judas son of James. They all joined together constantly in prayer, along with the women and Mary the mother of Jesus, and with his brothers. (Acts 1:13–14)

Peter motioned with his hand for them to be quiet and described how the Lord had brought him out of prison. "Tell James and the other brothers and sisters about this," he said, and then he left for another place. (Acts 12:17)

When they finished, James spoke up. "Brothers," he said, "listen to me. Simon has described to us how God first intervened to choose a people for his name from the Gentiles. The words of the prophets are in agreement with this, as it is written:

"'After this I will return and rebuild David's fallen tent.

Its ruins I will rebuild, and I will restore it, that the rest of mankind may seek the Lord, even all the Gentiles who bear my name, says the Lord, who does these things— things known from long ago.'

"It is my judgment, therefore, that we should not make it difficult for the Gentiles who are turning to God. Instead we should write to them, telling them to abstain from food polluted by idols, from sexual immorality, from the meat of strangled animals and from blood. For the law of Moses has been preached in every city from the earliest times and is read in the synagogues on every Sabbath." (Acts 15:13-21)

When we arrived at Jerusalem, the brothers and sisters received us warmly. The next day Paul and the rest of us went to see James, and all the elders were present. Paul greeted them and reported in detail what God had done among the Gentiles through his ministry.

When they heard this, they praised God. Then they said to Paul: "You see, brother, how many thousands of Jews have believed, and all of them are zealous for the law. They have been informed that you teach all the Jews who live among the Gentiles to turn away from Moses, telling them not to circumcise their children or live according to our customs. What shall we do? They will certainly hear that you have come, so do what we tell you. There are four men with us who have made a vow. Take these men, join in their purification rites and pay their expenses, so that they can have their heads shaved. Then everyone will know there is no truth in these reports about you, but that you yourself are living in obedience to the law. As for the Gentile believers, we have written to them our decision that they should abstain from food sacrificed to idols, from blood, from the meat of strangled animals and from sexual immorality." (Acts 21:17–25)

After that, he appeared to more than five hundred of the brothers and sisters at the same time, most of whom are still living, though some have fallen asleep. Then he appeared to James, then to all the apostles, and last of all he appeared to me also, as to one abnormally born. (1 Corinthians 15:6-8)

I saw none of the other apostles—only James, the Lord's brother. (Galatians 1:19)

James, Cephas and John, those esteemed as pillars, gave
me and Barnabas the right hand of fellowship when
they recognized the grace given to me. They agreed that
we should go to the Gentiles, and they to the circumcised. All they asked was that we should continue to
remember the poor, the very thing I had been eager to
do all along.

When Cephas came to Antioch, I opposed him
to his face, because he stood condemned. For before
certain men came from James, he used to eat with the
Gentiles. But when they arrived, he began to draw
back and separate himself from the Gentiles because he
was afraid of those who belonged to the circumcision
group. (Galatians 2:9-12)

James, a servant of God and of the Lord Jesus Christ,
To the twelve tribes scattered among the nations:
Greetings (James 1:1).

[The entire Epistle of James]

Resources & Further Reading

Barclay, William, *The Gospel of Matthew, Volume Two, Chapters 11–28—The Daily Study Bible*, (Welch, 1975).

Brettall, Robert, *A Kierkegaard Anthology*, (Oxford University, 1947).

Cole, R. A., *The Epistle of Paul to the Galatians—Tyndale New Testament Commentaries*, (Eerdmans, 1984).

Jackson, Janet L., *Jesus Didn't Fit In: Raising Nontraditional Children*, (WestBow, 1993).

Lewis, C. S., *Mere Christianity*, (MacMillan, 1952).

Marshall, I. Howard, *The Acts of the Apostles—Tyndale New Testament Commentaries*, (Eerdmans, 1980).

Morris, Leon, *Luke—Tyndale New Testament Commentaries*, (Eerdmans, 1984).

Ropes, James Hardy, *A Critical and Exegetical Commentary on the Epistle of St. James*, (Clark, 1916).

Shanks, Hershel and Ben Witherington III, *The Brother of Jesus: The Dramatic Story & Meaning of the First Archaeological Link to Jesus & His Family*, (Harper Collins, 2003).

Shepard, J. W., *The Christ of the Gospels*, (Eerdmans, 1938).

Tasker, R.V.G., *The General Epistle of James: An Introduction and Commentary—Tyndale New Testament Commentaries*, (Eerdmans, 1983).

Varner, William, *James—Evangelical Exegetical Commentary*, (Lexham, 2014).

www.ingramcontent.com/pod-product-compliance
Lightning Source LLC
Chambersburg PA
CBHW062050080426

42734CB00012B/2601